SURVIVAL, REVIVAL AND
MORAL REVOLUTION:
THE LIFE AND TIMES OF
ALEXANDER STEWART

SURVIVAL, REVIVAL AND MORAL REVOLUTION:

THE LIFE AND TIMES OF

ALEXANDER STEWART

SIMON WILLIAMS

Troubador Publishing Ltd
Unit E2 Airfield Business Park,
Harrison Road, Market Harborough,
Leicestershire. LE16 7UL
Tel: 0116 2792299
Email: books@troubador.co.uk
Web: www.troubador.co.uk

Paperback ISBN 978 1805143 604
Hardback ISBN 978 1805143 611

British Library Cataloguing in Publication Data.
A catalogue record for this book is available from the British Library.

Printed and bound in Great Britain by 4edge Limited
Typeset in 11pt Minion Pro by Troubador Publishing Ltd, Leicester, UK

To my grandchildren

James and Bella

Fran and Flo

Daisy, Stanley and Annie

If Alexander Stewart had not survived all those seventeen near-death experiences, where would we be?

CONTENTS

ACKNOWLEDGEMENTS

This book is about the life and times of Alexander Stewart. My first acknowledgement must be to him, to his extraordinary life, and to his decision to record its dramatic earlier stages for the benefit of his children. The fact that he decided to keep a diary record later on means that we can see the whole of his life from his perspective. We are indebted to Stewart's grandson, P. Malcolm Stewart, who took the decision to publish his record for private circulation amongst his family and friends. We must also be thankful that he invited Albert Peel to carry out this work. Peel was a historian of Congregationalism who was well able to appreciate and convey the significance of Stewart's life and work. Finally in this section on the source material, I am much indebted to my cousin, Rosalind Pearson, who has a keen interest in the history of the family. Ros studied Stewart's manuscript in the library of the Stewart Society in Edinburgh, from which she wrote *Alexander Stewart's Narrative of his Life* (2011). This concentrates in particular on his family life and the domestic challenges of bringing up a large family in an intensive working environment. It opened up a new perspective on the emotional dimension of Stewart's life and his relationships with his children. Ros has been most generous in passing on information and supporting what I have been doing.

The book seeks to set Alexander Stewart in the context of the often dramatic and turbulent times he lived through. Without the work of some marvellous historians, this task would have been quite beyond me. In particular, I am grateful to Linda Colley for her brilliant reading of the long eighteenth century; to David Bebbington and Stewart, J. Brown for their deeply insightful analyses of the religious dimension of nineteenth-century Britain; to Tom Devine and David Cannadine for their authoritative overviews of Scottish and British history, respectively; to Jonathan Parry for opening up my thinking about the Whigs and the Liberals; to Michael Taylor for his forensic analysis of the British Establishment's defence of slavery and what it took to defeat it; to George Kitson Clark and Andrea Wulf, across a span of sixty years, for making me think about the connections between Alexander Stewart and the Romantic movement; to David Newsome and Simon Heffer for their rich insights into the public school revolution; to John Morrill for enabling me to appreciate more fully the links between the Victorian Evangelicals and their Puritan predecessors; to Robert Allen, whose statistics on population and class steered me in the direction of understanding better the socio-economic dimension of the story; and to Timothy Larsen, whose PhD thesis highlighted the appeal of Nonconformity to the middle classes. As you will see from the Endnotes, there are many other historians whose work I have drawn on, and to whom I am indebted.

Many people have contributed to the process of turning all the above into a book and I am grateful to all of them. Creek Wier has made valiant and tolerant sense of all my disorganised rewrites and updates, producing a document which the book producers can readily work with. Sarah Burton from the Society of Authors has made it possible for me to navigate the challenging waters of self-publishing. Holly Porter and the team at Troubador have turned the bare and basic manuscript into a good-looking book with a combination of efficiency, friendliness and flair. Kevin Wilsher, from the Regency Society, and Lesley

Eastabrook, the Lancing College archivist, have generously given me permission to use their material without charge. The Sir Halley Stewart Trust and Duncan Stewart, in particular, have been most accommodating in enabling me to read and make full use of Alexander Stewart's manuscript. Matt Hobbs, my son-in-law, has adapted ingeniously Stewart's original map, showing his journey of captivity. Many thanks also to Marian Aird for demonstrating the importance of a high quality index.

I owe a particular debt to David Bebbington, Emeritus Professor of History at the University of Stirling. His commentary on an early draft was invaluable both in pointing out some inaccuracies and in giving me confidence about my interpretation of the historical events. Family and friends have shown a keen interest in the emerging book and given me encouraging feedback at various points along the way. Penny Bentley and Roger James have been my companions at every stage of the journey. They have provided an invaluable commentary throughout. As well as helping me improve the text, they have made me feel that the project is eminently worthwhile, and, in the event of any faltering on my part, is definitely worthy of completion! Thank you both very much.

Finally, I owe a huge debt to my wife, Daphne. I have done most of the work for the book in the last couple of years when preparing for, and recovering from, complex hip surgery. Without Daphne's unfailing support for the project (and myself!), any completion date might have receded into the far distance.

AUTHOR BIOGRAPHY

Simon Williams is the great-great-grandson of Alexander Stewart. He read history at Cambridge University, where his special subject was Oliver Cromwell. He taught history at various state schools in outer London before taking up the headship of Shene School (1986–97). He then moved into educational consultancy and was Chair of LEAD (Leading through Enquiry and Dialogue) from 2012–23. He has written two history books for schools, published by MacMillan: *China Since 1949* and *The Rise and Fall of Hitler's Germany*. He also co-authored *Leading and Managing Schools through Challenging Times*. Simon has two daughters and seven grandchildren. He lives in Teddington with his wife, Daphne.

A NOTE ON THE
THE MANUSCRIPT

The story of Alexander Stewart's life is based on the account he wrote for his children and the diary which he subsequently kept. All extracts from this manuscript are in italics without any additional reference to the source.

The author studying Alexander Stewart's manuscript.

ONE

WALKING AWAY FROM HOME

ONE DAY IN 1804

One day in 1804, Alexander Stewart, aged fourteen, left his house in Kirkcaldy, Scotland. Sometime during the day, he decided not to come back. He attached himself to a group of boys, probably not much older than him, who were running away from home to find work at sea. In their case, it was walking to Edinburgh; then sitting on top of an early morning coach to Sunderland; then scouring the local shipyards for work. He had not asked his parents' permission; had he done so, they would certainly have turned him down. His two elder brothers had just gone to sea with their parents' approval. Stewart records that his mother and father:

> *deeply grieved them and their laments over them I often heard… my parents very naturally felt a kind of increased interest in me, and, for the moment I was fully sensible of special manifestations of affection.*

Both parents came from families that had owned their own farm, going back generations. Stewart's grandfather on his father's side

1

left the land, *not being the eldest son*, and therefore not inheriting the farm. His parents settled in Kirkcaldy. Eleven miles north of Edinburgh, it was a busy port trading with the continent as well as being a centre of linen manufacturing, shipbuilding and ceramics.

1. *Stewart's family lived near the pottery chimneys shown in this 1838 painting of Kirkcaldy.*

It was here they brought up their twelve children in the Protestant faith. Stewart remembered being taunted by his elder brothers for learning the catechism better than them:

> *but always had my compensation in my Father's taking me between his knees, when answering them by the fireside on Sabbath evenings.*

Stewart was deeply attached to his parents. As he later struggled to explain why he walked out on them, he recorded:

> *no boy, as far as I can recollect my early emotions and history, could love them more.*

2

STEWART'S EARLY POLITICAL EDUCATION

His father had a lively, enquiring mind; a quality which he nurtured in Alexander:

I have many happy recollections of some of my father's occasional remarks and conversations... and the eloquent way in which he used to dwell on the stirring political topics of the day soon after the French Revolution, and while Bonaparte was preparing to invade England, as he stopped, at intervals, in reading the newspapers, as he daily did to a number of people who frequented our house for that purpose.

This level of popular interest in politics was widespread, as Tom Devine points out:

the Scottish population was one of the most literate in Europe and political ideas were increasingly disseminated widely through newspapers, pamphlets and broadsheets.[1]

Stewart's father and his friends would have had vigorous discussions about the relationship between England and Scotland. The Act of Union of 1707, linking Scotland to England and Wales, abolished the Scottish Parliament. It voted in favour of its own demise as a result of what Devine calls the English government's:

formidable political management machine... the promise of favours, sinecures, pension, offices and straightforward cash bribes became indispensable to ensure successive government majorities.[2]

Initially, the union was deeply unpopular in a country proud of its history of resisting invasion and conquest by the Plantagenet kings of England. Crucial to the successful passage of the Act was that Scotland retained its Presbyterian Church as the Church of Scotland. It also gained access to rapidly expanding English, now British, markets. Well before 1800, the benefits of the Union had become apparent: Great Britain formed the largest free trade area in Europe; after 1707, Scotland had access to the markets of the British Empire with plentiful opportunities for Scots to participate in empire building, whether as soldiers, doctors, engineers, missionaries or settlers. In addition, at the Battle of Culloden in 1746, the Protestant Union had finally seen off the Jacobite threat to restore the Catholic Stuart dynasty. A sense of dual identity was emerging with many Scots seeing themselves both as Scots and British, brought together through the powerful unifying thread of Protestantism.

So, the newspaper discussions, led by Alexander Stewart's father, would most likely have expressed very real concerns about the prospects of a Napoleonic invasion. As Linda Colley reminds us:

Napoleon's Army of England was by far the most formidable invasion force assembled against Great Britain up to that time, the threat it represented was a protracted one, and it came very close to succeeding.[3]

Stewart's father and friends may well have enthused about the French Revolution in its early stages, before the Reign of Terror and the declaration of war against Britain in 1793. In much of Scotland, the outbreak of the Revolution triggered demands for reform of parliament and, in particular, a widening of the franchise. Very few Scots had the vote (4,500 people out of a population of 2.3 million), and most of the small number of Scottish seats in Westminster were in the pocket of Henry Dundas, the supreme political fixer, known as King Harry the Ninth. Dundas was the British government's manager for Scotland, and he certainly managed most of the Scottish MPs in Westminster. By 1790, he was in control of thirty-four of the forty-one Scottish constituencies. With the danger from France, the issue of parliamentary reform was sidelined but did not go away.

2. Henry Dundas, 1st Viscount Melville; a figure of controversy, then and now.

3. The Melville Monument in Edinburgh. Reaching 150 feet tall, it was erected in 1821 through voluntary contributions from naval personnel. In 2021, Edinburgh Council placed a plaque on the monument stating that Melville was instrumental in delaying the abolition of the slave trade.

DISSATISFACTION WITH THE PRESBYTERIAN CHURCH

The enquiring mind of Alexander Stewart's father also extended to religion, where he and his family, like many Protestant Scots at the time, had rejected the national Presbyterian Church in favour of independent alternatives. His own brother was a deacon of the Independent Chapel in Kirkcaldy for more than fifty years.

From the mid 1750s, the Moderate Party within the Presbyterian Church had, in effect, taken control. Its members favoured the appointment of ministers by lay patrons, normally the local landowner, rather than the godly congregation. This was resisted bitterly by the godly congregations, who had numbers, but not clout, on their side. In addition, heavily influenced by the Scottish Enlightenment, the Moderates shifted the emphasis within the Church to its moral teachings. It was a world away from the fire-and-brimstone legacy of John Knox, who had attempted two hundred years earlier to turn the Scots, in Arthur Herman's words,

> *into God's chosen people, and Scotland into the New Jerusalem.*[4]

There is no evidence that Stewart's father wanted to return to that. Most likely, he did want something more full-bodied than what the Moderates were providing. For many Protestant Scots, the Church had become, according to Herman,

> *so refined and aloof from everyday life that it offered nothing to people who needed a strong emotional outlet... and an inner spiritual life.*[5]

EXPERIENCING THE EVANGELICALS

Alexander loved going with his father to worship in unconventional places:

> *the preaching was generally from a temporary pulpit in the church yard, while the audiance sat on the grass.*

Later on, he notes being:

> *present with my father in an upper room, attending the services conducted by one of Haldane's ministers, among the first visits these eminent men paid to Kirkaldy.*

Robert Haldane was a wealthy landowner who had become intensely concerned about what he and his brother, James, saw as the loss of faith in Scotland. They attributed this both to rapid industrialisation and population growth, and the effect of the Moderate Party. He sold his estates and spent his time and money preaching the gospel in upper rooms and open spaces, building chapels and training men for the ministry. He and his brother triggered a popular Evangelical revival, following on from George Whitefield's missionary campaign in Scotland in the 1740s.

Alexander Stewart lost his own faith in the prisons of France, but that experience of Evangelical preaching in the upper room stayed with him and may well have contributed to his own recovery of faith.

CONSEQUENCES

Alexander Stewart had a rich upbringing, experiencing his parents' love and his father's engagement with the world of politics and religion. Had he not walked out on that day in 1804, perhaps he would have become a minister in the local independent church in Kirkcaldy, taking a keen interest in the tumultuous politics of the age. As it was, much later in his life, he did become a minister in the Congregational Church of Barnet, taking a keen interest in the tumultuous politics of the age.

He did walk out that day in 1804, and that decision had momentous consequences. After running away to sea, Stewart was captured by the French off the coast of Brighton and was kept as a prisoner for ten years in often brutal conditions. During this time, he was marched something like 1,500 miles, mostly in chains, between different prisons. He made four attempts to escape. When he finally returned home in 1815 and asked his mother whether she knew him, she held his jacket quite tight, *as if she would not let me go again*, rolled up his left sleeve and pointed to a mark on his skin of which he had no knowledge. He never saw his beloved father again. He died of a fever in 1809, at the age of forty-nine, not knowing why his son had left home, or what had happened to him.

WHY?

So why did Stewart leave home? In his account, he says,

at an evil hour, through the persuasion of a dastardly fellow, I was induced to leave home by stealth, and to go to Sunderland for the purpose of going to sea... It was the decision of a moment, for I had not the least intention of such a thing when I left home that morning. O, the thoughtlessness of youth!

Very soon, he bitterly regretted what he had done:

I had not gone many miles before my heart failed me... Instead of mingling with the rest in their mirth, I wept bitterly... and yet I had not nerve to obey the instinctive promptings of my heart, and brave the ridicule of my companions to return. Night came and I went to bed, but no sleep for me. As I thought of my parents' anxiety about me, my sobbings were fearful. Nor was this by any means a transient feeling.

Alexander Stewart had decided on the spur of the moment to run away to sea. It was a decision that was to haunt him; it lost him the rest of his youth and caused him, as well as his family, much distress and suffering. Yet it was one that was ultimately to shape an extraordinarily rich and productive life.

TWO

CABIN BOY

Any romantic notion Stewart might have had about life at sea would soon have gone overboard. At Newcastle, he was forced to join a cargo ship carrying coal to London. As the cabin boy, he was at the bottom of the hierarchy and treated:

as if I had been a dog and a total stranger to the feelings of humanity.

There was no compassion, no friendly words. It was neglect or verbal abuse, and it was extremely dangerous. Before they had even left the River Tyne for the North Sea, Stewart had fallen overboard as he was throwing slops into the sea. Convinced he was drowning, he was rescued by the captain who jumped overboard, swam towards him, grabbed hold of his hair and pulled him to the surface.

On the third voyage, in a fierce storm near Brighton, the battered ship fell to pieces. Stewart survived first by clinging to the others and then, when they became separated, by hanging onto a pole belonging to the mast, which eventually washed up on the shore. On another voyage to Rochester, when they were unloading the coal, he took a wrong step and fell overboard. Again, he thought this was the end:

I distinctly remember holding up my hands under the water and looking up to Heaven, but cannot recollect what my feelings were... except the persuasion that I was dying.

On the journey back to Sunderland, as he was tacking the ship, the chains and pulley attached to the sail struck him on his head and he was knocked flat on the deck. He described what happened next:

After lying awhile on the deck unnoticed, the cook came and helped me up, but with a vile oath, and then sending me off as a lubber who had no business on board of ship. No one on board ever asked whether I was hurt or not, or took the least notice of what had happened to me.

On the next voyage to Plymouth, at last he had someone he could talk to. Graham had also run away to sea in the same group as Stewart. Loaded with coal, the boat sailed for Plymouth in the depth of winter. From infancy, Stewart *felt cold or heat on their first approach* very acutely. He described how he reacted on board:

I often suffered much from the cold, especially as my clothes were seldom dry. Neither Graham nor I had a sufficient supply of clothing to allow us to change when we got below, or into our hammocks, so that instead of sleeping and rest in bed, I used to shiver the whole watch, with my knees huddled up to my mouth and my teeth shollering most painfully.

They reached Plymouth Sound just as a severe storm set in. The captain cast anchor but that didn't stop them heading for the rocks. He cut the cables in an attempt to get round the notorious Devil's Point. A swell of the sea lifted them just in time to take them round the point. It was, the captain said afterwards, *a hairbreadth escape.* As for Stewart, the cold had so affected his hands that *I had little use of them for several days.*

THREE

PRISONER OF NAPOLEON

CAPTURE AND IMPRISONMENT

After Plymouth, the next voyage as cabin boy was his last. On 5th January 1805, Stewart's ship had just rounded Beachy Head and was approaching Brighton when what looked like a fishing vessel was seen coming towards them. It was, in fact, a French privateer, too fast for the boat carrying coal, which tried desperately to get within the protective range of the battery guns at Brighton. Stewart was up the mast trying to alter the sail when they opened fire, with many of the shots going through the sail under his feet. By the time he had scrambled back on the deck, a dozen men had boarded the boat, armed with pistols and cutlasses.

The crew was taken to Gravelines on the French coast and then marched to Dunkirk, tied to each other with rope, which Stewart likened to horses being driven to Smithfield Market:

> *We arrived in Dunkirk towards evening, on entering which our guard to our great annoyance, again beat their drums at our head, to summon the idle, the curious, and the simple, to witness French trophies of war.*

4. *The collier, in this engraving of 1814, is delivering coal to Brighton beach. Horses are taking the coal from ship to shore. Stewart was on similar boats near Brighton, when shipwrecked in 1804 and captured by the French in 1805.*

They were thrown into a large room in the town's prison, where bedding was chaff riddled with vermin, which they had to share with French prisoners. Stewart described them as:

abandoned in character as they were filthy in person, and wretched in circumstances.

On the fourth night, a fire was started by sparks from prisoners' smoking igniting the straw bedding. As they shouted for help, the guard refused to open the door, suspecting a plan to escape:

By this time the scene inside was appalling – all pressed towards the door to get what air they could. Numbers were trodden under foot and must have suffered much, if indeed all survived.

Finally, the guard let them out. Stewart fainted in the courtyard and found himself in a cell the following day with the ship's crew minus the French prisoners.

SARRELIBRE: THE OLD HOSPITAL

The prisoners were then marched five hundred miles to the fortified town of Sarrelibre. Tied together for the first four days, they walked twenty-five miles a day, mostly barefoot in Stewart's case as his shoes had fallen apart. He then spent a year and a half in a prison outside the town walls. It had been a hospital but was abandoned because of its unhealthy position. He was shut up in a large room with over fifty other prisoners. He was permanently hungry as the basic rations consisted of one pound of brown bread and nominally half a pound of meat, which was mostly offal and often rotten. He was living in one set of clothes, which was falling apart. There were no buttons, no pins, no soap. There was no work and nothing to do. Prisoners spent much of their time in or near their beds, gambling, drinking and often fighting. He did not remember seeing a book of any kind in the time he was there.

> There was no one who cared for me, not a creature to give me a hint of anything good, while a rapid tide of evil rolled me with the mass… I had to make my way as best I could, often distressed to melancholy… all was low, all was vulgar, all was debasing.

The one element of good that did come his way was the intervention of Philly the painter, who saved him from a cat-o'nine-tails flogging. One day, Stewart and another prisoner were alone as they were unwell, whilst the others attended the daily roll call outside. The prisoner came over to Stewart's bed

15

and took half his bread. Stewart told some of the others when they came back. The thief denied it. The prisoners set up their own court, which decided, as there was no proof on either side, the man's word should be taken rather than the boy's, *and that I should be flogged for accusing him*. At this point, Philly the painter, *to whom I had never spoken a word*, stood up and spoke in Stewart's defence:

> *He pleaded my case so well that the sentence was reversed, and the culprit well nigh put in my place.*

In the end, neither was punished but:

> *the wretched culprit could never after look me in the face... While in that place I lived to be able to hold up to contempt the reasoning of those who as judges at first condemned me in such style.*

What kept him going through this extended nightmare was his imagination, as he visualised the life outside in the shape of:

> *the thousand and one castles which I built in the air as I paced and repaced my short walk of about thirty feet long one weary day after another.*

SARRELIBRE: THE BARRACKS

After eighteen months, they were moved to the barracks inside the town. Here, conditions were better. They were in separate rooms, each accommodating fourteen prisoners. The food was no better, but each room had a separate fire and kettle, together with a tub for its own water. Unlike the old hospital, Stewart no longer felt isolated and on his own with nothing to do. He formed close relationships with several boys his own age. He wrote:

this intimacy, natural as it was in our circumstances, and much as it tended to relieve the hardships of a long prison life, I cannot now regard with unmingled feelings, for it left plague spots on the memory.

He was particularly close to one boy. They were evenly matched in athletic prowess and so were encouraged by the prisoners to compete against each other for prizes of apples in running and wrestling competitions. One day, his friend was bribed to join Napoleon's Irish Brigade and Stewart could have easily followed him. He wrote later:

I could scarcely endure the separation... my associations with that youth I can never forget.

Stewart also now had opportunities to better himself and satisfy his thirst for learning. He earned extra money by cleaning their room and washing people's clothes. He used it to buy some clothes for himself. Later, he used some of this money to pay for lessons when the authorities opened schools funded by voluntary contributions from England. His teacher was a man called McCaa. According to Stewart, he was no linguist. He knew very little of his own language and cared as little. But he was a skilled teacher of writing, arithmetic and navigation. Stewart soaked all this up, especially navigation, and it wasn't long before McCaa was paying him as his helper.

There were books in the barracks but no sign of the Bible. Sunday was no different from any other day, except that some prisoners put on clean shirts. In this respect, the barracks didn't differ much from the old hospital. Not surprisingly, this was affecting Stewart:

Immorality in many important respects had a full swing among us... I remember the case of one individual reproving a profane oath on one occasion, but all instantly cried him down, and what distresses me most is that I sided with them.

FOUR

ESCAPE AND CAPTURE

SARRELIBRE: ESCAPE

Early in 1811, Stewart hatched a bold plan to escape. He was now twenty and had been in prison for six years. There was no sign of the war ending. Indeed, although he would not have known this, the French Empire was at its greatest extent. Napoleon controlled nearly all of Europe except for the Balkans. Stewart was, in his words,

> *weary beyond all endurance of a continued prison life, and naturally sighing night and day, as I advanced in my teens, to be on the broad stage of human life.*

His escape plan was to go over the wooden fencing on top of the parapet walls on the ramparts and slide down to the ground outside using a sixty-foot rope. He persuaded three other prisoners to join him. It took six weeks to make the rope, during which time he kept it hidden under his hat. They waited for a day with thick snow when the guards stayed in their sentry boxes.

It was about eleven o'clock. My nerves were fully braced.
"Now for it," I exclaimed – "now or never." "It is madness"
said Murray. "They will see you when on the top of the
pailings, you'll be shot, you may depend on it." "I'll follow
you," said Graham "if you go, though I think we had better
wait a little longer." Squires said not a word. "Now or
never," I said, "Here I go, if I go alone."

As he came down, he twisted the rope round and round in his
hand. He landed with the flesh torn off his hand and the bones
visible. The others came down after him. They got through the
defences of the town and were in open country when they heard
gunfire from the barracks, signalling that prisoners had escaped.
Before long, local peasants, scenting reward, were pursuing
them, armed with sticks and pikes. They ran for three hours
before they got to the banks of the Moselle. It was frozen. With
the peasants still in pursuit, they faced an existential choice:
surrender and an unpleasant fate in store, or drowning if the ice
cracked. They took the risk of drowning. The ice held, and they
taunted the peasants on the other side.

But where now? The French were in control of all the
territory up to the English Channel. It seems the plan was simply
to avoid capture. A German-speaking farmer and his family
took them in for a night. They provided them with food, brandy,
beds to sleep in and dressings for Stewart's badly injured hand,
showing a kindness and warmth he never forgot. After they left
the farmhouse, they survived for seven days, walking at night
and finding somewhere to sleep during the day, before they were
spotted and seized by a posse of gendarmes.

Treated as *mauvais sujets*, they were sent to Verdun in
chains. Stewart's right hand was in a sling around his neck, his
left hand was chained so tightly that he needed help in eating,
drinking and what he called *other respects*. It was the middle of
winter. His shoes had given way, and his bare feet were bleeding

from the sharp stones on roads in very poor condition, which were turning from frost into mud. After four days of intense discomfort and pain from both hand and feet, Stewart and the others reached Verdun. From there, they were ordered to the fortress of Bitche, not far from Strasbourg, whose name, according to Stewart, *struck terror into the hearts of all the English prisoners in France.* When they got to Metz, the main city of Lorraine, Stewart was admitted to the hospital as his hand *had now become frightful and smelt very bad.* The doctors were very concerned about his condition. After much consultation, they asked for his consent to amputate his hand:

I pleaded hard with them, even with tears when the senior surgeon present said to the others "Tachons, il est encore bien jeune." (Let us try on, youth is in his favor). This was a happy word for me. I could have kissed the old doctor.

Gradually his hand got better, although he was hardly able to use it for a year and felt pain in the cold for the next twenty years or so.

BITCHE

In chains in the intense heat of the summer of 1811, Stewart made the march to Bitche. The prisoners there were a mixture of deserters, criminals, officers and intellectual opponents of Napoleon. His group was put with the deserters and criminals, confined to the underground quarters built into the rock where the walls dripped with water. As well as being damp, the place was overcrowded, dark and extremely uncomfortable. Here, they were shut up every night and for three hours in the middle of the day. The others in the barrack rooms on ground level were in much better accommodation. Stewart did manage to make contact with some of them, from whom he borrowed books, reading in French, as best as he could, works of Voltaire, Mirabeau and Rousseau. For the most part, however, he was confined below where the conditions were as bad as they had been in the old hospital at Sarrelibre:

> *The whole was tedious, wearing and depressive beyond what I could well describe. The frequent boisterous rioting, gambling, drinking, swearing and fighting... often made the place a little hell on earth.*

After nine months or so, Stewart's situation changed very much for the better. He and a few others, chosen by the commandant, were moved to the barrack rooms where, in his words, *I was brought into better society than I had ever before enjoyed.* It was from there that he saw Napoleon's troops marching eastwards towards Russia in the early summer of 1812:

> *It seemed to us that the train was interminable. The chain seemed unbroken for many hours of every day, and for weeks in succession. The thing electrified our jailors, and equally depressed us. The sound was ever echoing in our ears "The Emperor will soon subdue England."*

Napoleon seemed impregnable. There was no prospect of escape from Bitche. Stewart's youth was disappearing. When the authorities asked for prisoners to go to Briançon in the Alps, Stewart volunteered, even though it involved a march of eight hundred miles in chains and was going in the opposite direction of home. Early in 1813, he set off in a detachment of thirty or so prisoners, chained by the neck, which was much more restrictive and uncomfortable than hand chains. He wrote:

It was but rarely that those in charge of us would loosen anyone to attend to any of the calls of nature.

Stewart was fortunate to survive the march. Near Lyons, he was struck down by a virulent fever, probably caused by having to sleep in damp clothes. He was so ill that he had to be carried from the jail in Lyons to the hospital in a barrow. Whatever or whoever contributed to his survival, he knew that it was not the Catholic priest in hospital who had offered to hear his confession for five francs and was prepared to be beaten down to two: an incident that only served to confirm Stewart's view of the Roman Catholic religion.

FIVE

ESCAPE AND FREEDOM

BRIANÇON

Briançon was a formidable fortress in the Alps, built by Napoleon on elevated ground beyond the town to guard the pass into Italy. Its granite walls were six-feet thick. It was too cold for glass windows, *hence we only had paper panes which had been previously steeped in oil.* Now it was full of prisoners, mainly those captured in Spain. Stewart and his fellow prisoners were in separate barracks, confined to rooms with a dozen or so others. He described his roommates as:

> *a profane old soldier, several old sailors of disagreeable tempers and two avowed infidels, who were familiar with the writings of Volney and Tom Paine.... Here I imbibed not a few of their sentiments... and came at last even to pride myself on rising above the prejudices and priestly fetters of religion.*

Briançon, in Stewart's eyes, was even worse than Bitche. The material conditions were as bad; food was no better. There was no soap. To wash their shirts, they soaked them in urine gathered in the tub before washing them under the pump. Their treatment was, in Stewart's words:

barbarous… running throughout a full year without our going outside of the room to attend to the common claims of nature.

In terms of the inmates' own behaviour, the bullies ruled the roost. That is until a provoked Stewart took on *the dictator of his own room, and the terror of others.* One day, he started to push Stewart around. Stewart dared him to touch him again:

On which he struck me forthwith. On this I stripped and challenged him. This led to a regular fight. The room was cleared, all got upon the beds to leave us and our seconds the middle of the room. It was a long and hard struggle, but I came off quite triumphant, to the surprize and I may say the gratification of all present seeing I was but a stripling compared with him. This fact raised my fame in a new way; I myself was not a little proud of it. I was often treated with drink, etc., by many who before scarcely ever spoke to me. This again led to other contests of a similar kind, whose fame intoxicated my vain mind.

Stewart was still determined to escape. Ingeniously, on his third attempt, he found a way. The first effort didn't get beyond his room. He teamed up with Midshipman Hare to create an opening in the back wall, but the guards heard them tapping. They were sent for forty days to the tiny, dark punishment cell on bread and water, where they used others in the cell to help create a diversion, which enabled them to slip out.

They escaped from the fortress, but this was very different from the open countryside around Sarrelibre. They survived one night in the bitter cold of the Alps on brandy, which they had managed to take with them, before they were captured. The commandant paraded them in front of the troops and prisoners where *he came up close to me, pulled his beard with rage, foamed at the mouth and gnashed his teeth* before accusing Stewart of writing a letter to the authorities in Paris complaining of the conditions in the prison. Stewart responded by saying, in French, *"Sir, submission is unavoidable where there is overwhelming force."*

This inflamed his rage to perfect madness... he ran and unscrewed one of the soldier's bayonets, brandished it about my head, and at last pricked me in the back, which though it bled a good deal, made no very serious wound. I believe, however, that the mark still remains on my shoulder.

On the third attempt, Stewart used deception to outwit the commandant and get right away from Briançon and the Alps. He found out that a special group of two hundred prisoners were to be sent to Arras in the north of France. With money and clothes, he bribed one of the group to change places with him. The day before they left, by arrangement with Stewart, some of these prisoners rushed at him and a companion as they left their room to empty the tub. During the melee, he changed places with the man he had bribed. Next morning, as they assembled in front of the commandant for their final roll-call, Stewart, with discoloured hair and coal dust on his face, dressed in a ragged jacket and an old cap, answered to the name of Benjamin West. The commandant gave the order to march, the drums beat, the gates opened and Stewart's heart leapt for joy.

ARRAS

In the time between Stewart observing the Napoleonic army marching to Moscow at Bitche and walking out of the fortress at Briançon, the situation in Europe had been completely transformed. The invasion of Russia was a disaster. Approximately 550,000 troops had set out. Only 120,000 or so came back. The Allies were closing in on Napoleon as Stewart marched northwards.

5. *Napoleon's army of 500,000 men cross the Neman River and invade Russia in June 1812.*

Napoleons Rückzug aus dem brennenden Moskau.

6. *Napoleon withdraws from Moscow in September 1812. Earlier, he had entered the city to find it deserted. It was then set on fire.*

7. *Tegg's caricature shows the Napoleonic army ragged and starving, retreating across a frozen landscape strewn with corpses and dead or dying horses.*

This was a very different march from the ones he was used to. He could walk freely, talk to whoever he liked and marvel at some of the magnificent scenery which he had been deprived of for so long. His ease of manner and knowledge of French, which he had been acquiring in the various prisons, meant that the French officers used him to communicate with the prisoners, help distribute food and organise the overnight accommodation. Instead of infested jails, they were staying in stables, haylofts and convents, or being billeted on the local population.

After six weeks, they reached Arras. They were placed in barracks where the conditions were much better than any he had experienced. Each prisoner had space, privacy and opportunities to exercise, worship and attend classes:

> *It soon got abroad that I knew something of the French language; I was consequently urged to form a French class. I complied and did well with it.*

Two months after his arrival, the commandant found out that Stewart had translated a petition from the prisoners to the minister of war in Paris. He summoned Stewart to his office. After his experience with the commandant at Briançon, Stewart expected the worst. He was trembling from head to foot and his knees were knocking. Instead, the commandant asked him if he had the time, with all his French teaching, to help him with administration and liaison with the prisoners. In effect, Stewart became his secretary, a full-time role, which meant he had to give up his teaching. He became very friendly with the commandant:

Early in the year 1814 news reached the depot that the allied armies of England, Russia and Prussia were approaching those borders of France which were nearest us… While sitting with him, one evening, in general conversation, he asked me if I had heard the news. I said 'Yes.' 'And I am glad of it' said he, saying which he pulled out of his coat pocket the Burbon Cockade, the 'Fleur de Lis', for he was a royalist at heart. 'We shall have the King – you'll soon be in England, mais n'en dites rien maintenant.' A few nights after this he took me to the opera, to hear a humorous piece just got up to ridicule the rule of Bonaparte, but under the name of Poor Nicholas.

ST MALO

As the Allies advanced into France, the prisoners were ordered to go further west under supervision that was becoming looser and looser. When they reached Rennes, Stewart and three others, one of whom was Graham from his cabin boy days, decided to break away and head for home via St Malo on the Channel coast. On the last full day before they got there, they ran and walked nearly thirty miles in less than six hours. When they saw the sea, they celebrated with brandy and *many hearty cheers*. When he boarded an English fighting ship in the harbour, after ten years as a prisoner of Napoleon, he was free at last.

Map showing Stewart's journey of captivity as prisoner of Napoleon 1805-14. For ease of reference, the modern boundaries of France have been used

SIX

HOMECOMING

BACK ON BRITISH SOIL

The joy of Stewart and his companions about being back on British soil was short-lived as they confronted the harsh reality of their situation. They had little money, no prospects and no support from the authorities or interest in their story. They decided to walk to London. They had just enough money for bread and cheese and very basic accommodation. With hairy knapsacks and peculiar-shaped straw hats, many took them to be French, which did not endear them to the local population. Stewart felt very bitter about their treatment:

> *I already felt I could spit in the face of England and abandon it for ever. We were not culprits. We did not occasion the war. Such treatment was insult added to injury. It was barbarous that we should be dispatched from the Guardship, and taken no notice of by the Portsmouth authorities in the first instance, not only as to our reaching our respective homes, but as to whether we could get a morsel of bread.*

Their first night in London was spent on boards in the taproom of a public house. They couldn't afford their beds. Two members of the party of four went their separate ways, leaving Stewart and Graham desperately looking for work, living off very basic rations. Stewart had to sell his precious books he had carried in his knapsack over much of France. He sold his shirts and handkerchiefs as well. He was too ashamed to go home, instead writing to his mother to say he was safe and living in London, but not revealing where he was staying:

I feared a letter from her. I felt she might conquer my purpose and induce me to return home, for I knew she exercised a kind of spell over all her family.

After five weeks or so, Stewart persuaded the captain of a ship going to St Petersburg to take him and Graham on. The ship had a special passenger, an envoy of the Emperor Alexander, who, with the other victorious leaders, were attending a conference in London after the first overthrow of Napoleon. The Russian officer had little English. Stewart would communicate with him in French. Before they set sail, Stewart again encountered the resident bully. This time it was the ship's cook:

He was cock of the walk on board – nobody dare gainsay him. One day he went so far as to take me by the shoulders and push me with his foot. I told him I once was a cabin-boy and suffered much from such vulgar fellows as he, but that day was gone by; saying this, I turned on him and gave him a real good thrashing, to the satisfaction of all on board, the Captain himself not excepted.

RUSSIA

In 1804, as cabin boy, Stewart had no one to talk to. When he set sail for Russia ten years later, much of the journey was spent in conversation. When he wasn't painting or doing other jobs on the boat, he was in discussion with the Russian officer or asking questions of the Methodist carpenter, out of earshot of the godless crew. When they reached Kronstadt, the Russian officer left the ship, which remained there until they had discharged their cargo and replaced it with timber for the voyage home. This required transferring the cargo onto the smaller boats that were needed for the narrow passage to St Petersburg, twenty miles away. This took some time and Stewart spent much of it in St Petersburg, where he marvelled at its palaces, monuments and cathedrals which *equalled, if they did not surpass in grandeur, any I had seen in France.*

Whilst Stewart was absorbing the rich potential and possibilities of a life from which he had been excluded for so long, the Russian expedition was also a reminder of the risks and dangers of life at sea. From Kronstadt, he set out with some of the crew for St Petersburg in one of the smaller boats. In the middle of a narrow passage, they met a well-manned Russian boat, which insisted they gave way:

> *We, as if masters of the seas everywhere, insisted that they should.*

During the ensuing fight, Stewart fell overboard and was in danger of being drowned under the boats as there was very little space to get to the surface for breath:

> *The Russians, to their credit, most honourably did all they could to get me into the boat, and then on board of our own ship. We all parted good friends.*

The crew was extraordinarily fortunate to survive the journey home. The captain's approach to danger was based on past experience (he had no knowledge of navigation theory and resisted Stewart's offer of help) and quantities of grog. When a violent storm arose as they got near the island of Bornholm, the captain refused to reef the sails, as the other ships were doing:

> *He paced the deck rapidly with his lame leg, pressed his hat firm on his head... calling the steward to bring him more grog... The oldest of the sailors trembled, for the captain was more than half insane with his grog... at this moment a heavy sea carried away our Quarter Boards, swept the deck of most of the spars, while we could save ourselves only by clinging to the rigging with our hands, while our legs were carried away with the sea.*

They managed to get safely around the island, but with much of their cargo lost. They soon reached Elsinore in Denmark when a small group, including Stewart and the captain, transferred to a rowing boat in order to pay the toll on Danish soil. By the time they returned to their boat, loaded now with Danish gin, a ferocious wind got up, which threatened to take them out to the North Sea. In the gathering dark, the others on the cargo ship saw what was happening and sent out a buoy, using all the cordage, to reach them. The captain and his group seized it and were pulled to safety. Faced with more contrary winds as they crossed the North Sea:

> *Now again the captain took to his cups, for he also had his supply of Hollands (gin). The second officer was as constant at his. They both drank very freely, – indeed they were seldom quite sober.*

The second officer's judgement proved better than the captain's, who was convinced they were heading for the Yorkshire coast. His number two insisted they were much further north and the hills they could see were the Cheviots. Stewart was back near his birthplace, but again he didn't go home. Instead, he stayed with the captain, returned to London and then came back north with another cargo of coal. One evening on shore, he was seized by a press gang and thrown on board a Guardship:

Now I criminated myself for not leaving the ship, when she reached the Thames, then in my heart cursed England, and wished I had entered the Russian service; or that I had never returned to England from France, but accepted one of the several tempting offers I had to make that country my home. I dreaded the very idea of being for life doomed to follow the sea, and in the service of a country for which I had already suffered ten years' imprisonment, and when I returned was sent to beg my bread, without thanks or sympathy.

The captain found out where he was and, with some difficulty, secured his release. Stewart went back to London again. He used his pay to buy some clothes and a ticket for his passage to Leith. This time he was going home.

SEVEN

SURVIVAL AND BEYOND

TWO QUESTIONS

In reflecting on Stewart's extraordinary experience, two questions present themselves: first, how did he manage to survive all the numerous occasions when he could have lost his life? Second, what qualities did he demonstrate that enabled him not only to survive but eventually to flourish? What light does his account throw on both these questions?

SURVIVAL

Three of Stewart's brothers went to sea. All died young as a result. Robert, the eldest son, was killed boarding an American privateer in the American War of 1812. George, the second eldest, died of yellow fever in the West Indies shortly after Robert. William drowned at sea with all the ship's crew off the coast of Norway in 1817. Other siblings died young of disease: two of consumption, one of typhus. The average age of death in Scotland around 1800 was just under forty. Between 1804 and 1815, there were at least seventeen occasions when Alexander

Stewart was close to losing his life. Remarkably, he survived them all and lived to the grand age of eighty-four.

Drowning at sea was the biggest threat to his survival. He fell overboard three times: in the River Tyne, in Rochester and in Kronstadt. His ship was wrecked or nearly wrecked three times: off Brighton, Plymouth and Bornholm. At Elsinore, the rowing boat very nearly went under in the North Sea.

After drowning, Stewart was most at risk from illness and death brought on by the conditions both in prison and on the chained marches. At Sarrelibre, he came out in a rash, which took the unhygienic form of a scab from ear to ear. According to the doctor, if Stewart had not ripped it off, it might have killed him.

At Bitche, an outbreak of scarlet fever carried off everyone who had it, except for Stewart. According to the doctor, Stewart was the only one whose nose bled.

Finally, there was the risk of being killed by the enemy. He was nearly shot when the French privateers were closing in on the cargo ship near Brighton. Once captured, he put his own life at risk every time he attempted to escape. In the epic break out from Sarrelibre, he could have been shot by the prison guards or later by the gendarmes, or cudgelled to death by the pursuing French peasants, or drowned if the ice had cracked on the river. Or he might have died of infection and blood poisoning from his hand, badly injured as he slithered down the rope in the great escape. This would have been made more likely if he had not dissuaded the surgeons at Metz from amputation, or indeed if they had not consulted him and then listened to his pleading.

Any one of these situations could have finished him off. As it was, he managed to survive eleven years spent in what were then two of the most life-threatening situations possible: boats, where he started and finished, and prisons in between. It does seem miraculous that he did survive, and Stewart thought it was. He attributed both his trials and tribulations and his survival to divine providence or God's intervention. He saw it as:

the hand at the helm… a man's heart deviseth his ways, but the Lord directeth his path.

Initially, it was an *Avenging Providence*:

though God may have forgiven me, yet in retributive justice he has ever since visited my iniquity with stripes; among which is that arrangement of his Providence, by which he has determined I shall spend my life far removed from the affectionate family I so wantonly deserted.

As Stewart made every effort to atone for his sin, so providence provided what he described as *marvellous support* and *overwhelming kindness*. It was this guiding hand that pulled him through.

STEWART'S ATTRIBUTES

Looking at the totality of these eleven years, what did enable Stewart not only to survive but also to make use of his experience to such good effect in his later life? This was the time when he was leaving childhood, going through adolescence and emerging into manhood. In what were often brutal conditions, where bullying was rife, how easy it would have been to have followed the herd in the struggle for survival, or perhaps to have given up hope altogether.

Four aspects of his character stand out: his moral compass and courage; his innate curiosity and thirst for learning; his resilience; and his emotional intelligence. All played their part in enabling Stewart both to survive and eventually flourish.

THE MORAL DIMENSION

Stewart had a strong sense of right and wrong. In the godless environment of cargo ships and prisons, he lost the religion of his family childhood but held on to the morality of the New Testament, as it had been expounded by the ministers and practised by his parents. This played a key part in sustaining him, when those around him were living according to a very different set of values. In his account, he gave two examples of where, much to his later shame, he joined in with the mob shouting down individual prisoners who were behaving according to their conscience. They seem to be exceptional deviations from his general pattern of behaviour. He also provided two examples, one in prison, one on the boat to Russia, where he showed great courage in challenging the bullies. His physical prowess meant he could take them on and defeat them in the only language they knew.

CURIOSITY AND THIRST FOR LEARNING

Stewart's curiosity and thirst for learning enabled him to look beyond his immediate closed environment, to ask searching questions about the world outside and seize every opportunity to acquire knowledge and understanding of it. These traits were much in evidence before he ran away:

> *My mother often used to tell me before the rest of the family, after I returned from France, how very fond I was of books when a mere child, and how I was remarked for giving my pence for them, in preference to anything else. In harmony with this I distinctly remember having a very strong desire to learn English Grammar, and that I much envied a boy I knew, who went to a school where it was*

taught, while I did not. Soon after this, another boy and I planned a new language, as we thought, many of whose odd combinations of sound and meaning I still remember.

Whilst in prison, he used every opportunity to acquire or borrow books and engage in conversations with anyone who had knowledge: whether about philosophy, navigation, English grammar or French. His determination to learn the French language served at least three purposes. First, he could begin to get into the leading thinkers of the French Enlightenment. Second, it helped him build relationships with his captors and so take on liaison roles between the French officers and the British prisoners. Finally, he was able to use it to take French classes, earning him money and providing him with a taste for teaching.

RESILIENCE

It is difficult to imagine a greater test of resilience than the one that confronted Stewart over such a long period. His life inside prison was debilitating and sapping. Marching long distances in chains tested his physical and mental capacity to the limit. A graphic example of this resilience was his account of what happened when the four captured escapees from Sarrelibre were being marched, tightly chained, towards Verdun. One of them, Murray, collapsed and could not get to his feet. The others were alarmed that he would be left in the road; Graham and Squires provided help but soon had to give up. Stewart had one arm in a sling and on the other side his hand was chained:

I then said to the Gendarmes – "If you will unchain my hand, I will try and carry him on my back." This was agreed to. But I soon found I could not carry him far

without resting. By doing that often, however, I managed
my task (of getting to the next town) in about an hour.

His resilience, partly at least, came from his growing knowledge of an exciting world outside, which he was determined to experience and contribute towards. He allied this with imaginative thinking and practical strategies for escaping to this world. Finally, when others might be hesitating, he acted, as he did when he took the lead in going over the wall at Sarrelibre.

EMOTIONAL INTELLIGENCE

During his period of imprisonment, Stewart became skilled at building relationships with others, both fellow prisoners and French officers. The foundation stone for this attribute was his awareness of both his own emotions and needs and those of others. One story in his account shows that this sensitivity (and kindness) was very much in evidence early on in his life:

A little girl was at fault one day in school. Our master called her up, but evidently wishing to get out of the necessity of punishing her, pleasantly said – 'If anyone will stand responsible for her better conduct in future, I will let her go.' On this I stood up and said I would; when there arose no small merriment in the school, the master himself taking his full share in it. I immediately felt ashamed, held down my head for most of the morning, and on coming out of school, ran home to avoid the banter of my schoolfellows.

On several occasions, he wrote about his own need for someone to show him kindness and compassion, and how desolate he was made to feel when that was not forthcoming. He made sure that these qualities underpinned, wherever possible, his own relationships. His closest friend was Frank Finn, whom he met on the march north in 1814. At Angers, Finn was taken to hospital with a fever. The other prisoners were given the order to march to Normandy:

I went to the hospital and told him the news, but oh, I shall never forget how he caught hold of me and begged of me to use my influence to take him with us, and not leave him helpless among strangers... I saw the doctors on the subject, but they said he could not be removed with safety. I returned and told Frank what they said, when he renewed his importunities with increased feelings. I need not say how much my own feelings were moved in all of this. I then resolved to go to the Commandant, into whose favor, by this time, I had made considerable advance. From him I got a letter to the doctors, in which he kindly and unexpectedly engaged to get Frank a conveyance, if he was not able to walk. This succeeded. Frank immediately left the hospital and gradually recovered.

What is striking about this account is the depth of emotion expressed by both Finn and Stewart, the latter's determination to resolve the situation and rescue his friend, and his success in doing so as a result of the relationship he had built with the commandant. As they moved north from Briançon, there were plenty of other examples where Stewart used his new liaison role to benefit the prisoners. At Arras, where they stayed for some time, *with a word I could get numbers of the prisoners liberty to go into town for the day.* When they were on the march, Stewart was able to work with the mayor or the local officials to ensure that food and lodgings were allocated efficiently and fairly.

EIGHT

A POLITICAL EDUCATION

FRANCE

As Stewart's living conditions in the French prisons improved, he was able to see more of French society and begin to make value judgements, which would have drawn on those conversations his father led over the newspapers. As we saw, much of that discussion was about Napoleon and the imminence of possible invasion. It may well have echoed the cartoonist James Gillray's 1803 view of Napoleon being roasted over a fire by the devil with the caption: *The Corsican Pest or Belzebub going to supper.* It was a sentiment Alexander Stewart, with his first-hand exposure to the Napoleonic regime, would have strongly agreed with:

> *It was in France, I very naturally sucked in the first elements of that perfected hatred of all tyranny which I have felt through life.*

Stewart also acquired direct experience of his other bête noire: the Roman Catholic Church. Observing the Catholic clergy in action confirmed his thinking that the Roman Catholic interpretation

The CORSICAN·PEST ; or BELZEBUB going to Supper.

8. The Corsican Pest or Belzebub going to Supper.
Here, James Gillray in 1803 portrays Beelzebub, the Prince of Devils, about to
fork the dimunitive Napoleon into the flames. The devil imps are holding their
noses against his stench. One of the verses below describes Napoleon as 'French
evil overflowing from his Head to his Toes.'

of Christianity was based on false promises and superstitious thinking. On the march to Bitche in prolonged summer heat:

the drought was fearful, and prayer for rain was very
general. We often saw immense trains of catholics, mostly

females, going in procession, led by their priests praying for
rain, preceded by immense candles, burning and melting
under the burning sun.

Later on, when the priest was trying to extract money from him for his confession, Stewart recorded in his account:

Here he uttered or muttered a few words in Latin, what,
no doubt, he meant as a prayer, but which seemed to me
like the jargon jugglers employ when they commence their
conjuring.

BRITAIN

In sharp contrast, Britain was a Protestant nation with parliamentary government. Belief in liberty protected by Parliament was fundamental to Stewart's thinking. However, this did not stop him from being highly critical of some key aspects of British society and identifying areas where he thought that Britain had much to learn from France. Britain was dominated by the aristocracy. Entry to its ranks from people with sufficient wealth was welcomed provided that the newcomers endorsed its values. In Stewart's eyes, these consisted, in part at least, of an indifference to the ranks below, as long as they presented no threat to those above. His treatment when back home formed his view that the indifference, bullying and coarse behaviour he had been exposed to in French prisons was an exaggerated microcosm of how people in England behaved.

What he appreciated about Napoleon's rule was, first, his insistence on opening up opportunities to all regardless of their rank in society. He referred to that:

deep feeling which sympathises but little with aristocratic gradations in society, while it can fully respect talents, morals, and experience.

Second, along with getting talented people into office came the provision of effective structures of government and the insistence on responsibility and competency. When Stewart and his fellow prisoners arrived each evening in the next village or town en route, the French officer contacted the mayor or official in charge to make the necessary arrangements. Back in England, for ex-prisoners on the winning side, there was no one to contact and there was no one who cared. Finally, there was Stewart's own experience of being treated as an equal by many of the French elite he came into contact with. One officer on the march north:

evidently wished to converse with me. We then talked very freely on a great variety of subjects and almost became intimate. He took wine with me the first time I offered it, and soon returned the compliment.

Stewart also recorded his experience of the French doctors in Metz hospital, when they were considering whether to amputate his hand:

They asked me very particularly how it felt, and then consulted together for some time, after which they very kindly remonstrated with me to consent to have it taken off. They might, indeed, have done it very unceremoniously without a word with me, but politeness and generosity especially towards foreigners prevailed in that colossal establishment.

SUMMARY

After all his varied experiences, Stewart's thinking about politics was both clear and nuanced. It wasn't a simple matter of Britain good and France bad. Parliamentary government was vital to prevent tyranny, but the franchise needed to be extended to avoid an aristocratic ruling class blocking a society based on merit and talent.

On the question of religion, he hadn't made up his mind. His Scottish, Protestant view of Roman Catholicism had been emphatically confirmed by what he had seen in France. Roman Catholic belief in the absolute authority of the Pope and the priestly hierarchy made it, so it seemed to Stewart, the ideal bedfellow for tyrannical emperors and monarchs. What should be there in its place – if anything? There was still much for him to ponder and resolve.

NINE

TEACHING

LEAVING KIRKCALDY

What was Stewart to do now? Despite the rich learning acquired from his harrowing experience in France, he had had, at the age of twenty-five, in the words of Albert Peel,

> *little education in the ordinary sense of the word… he had*
> *received neither the academic nor the technical training to*
> *fit him for profession or craft.*[6]

What he did have was knowledge of French and navigation, and both, as it turned out, were in demand in Kirkcaldy. He also had limited but rewarding experience of teaching. Before long, he was teaching French to schoolmasters and, separately, to some of the young ladies of the town. In the winter, the former cabin boy taught navigation to a class of sailors and sea captains as they waited for the better weather to set sail for Greenland or the Baltic.

Stewart could have stayed in Kirkcaldy. That is certainly what his mother and the rest of the family wanted. He applied for the post of Master at the Parochial School, run by the Presbyterian

Church of Scotland. He was turned down. According to his account, it was because he was falsely tainted with being a dissenter. That rejection confirmed his view of the Presbyterian Church. It also contributed to his decision to leave Kirkcaldy for London. Encouraged by letters from a fellow former prisoner, Baker, who was teaching in Egham, Stewart overcame his mother's resistance and returned to London – this time to teach.

TO LONDON TO TEACH

Over the next three years, Stewart taught in three very different schools in what turned out to be a highly effective, self-directed apprenticeship in teaching. When he started, his knowledge of the curriculum was limited to French, arithmetic and writing; his experience of teaching boys was virtually non-existent; and he had, what would have been for his classes, a strange half-French and half-Scottish accent. Against this, he did have extraordinary life experiences to draw on and, with these in mind, he applied to a school agent to secure him a teaching post.

He found a very different educational set-up in England to the one he had experienced as a boy, where there was a uniform system of provision. In Scotland, both parish and burgh had a legal responsibility to provide education, which in the parishes was subsidised through a tax on the local landowners. The Presbyterian Church upheld standards in schools, designed to ensure that, at the very least, parishioners could read the Bible and answer the catechism.

In England, the working class either had a very rudimentary education in the basics through dame schools or Sunday schools, or nothing at all. In 1800, nearly half the adult population of England could not sign their name. As J.F.C. Harrison points out:

The root cause of illiteracy was inadequate elementary education.[7]

Roy Porter describes what was on offer as:

A pot-pourri of distinct sorts of schoolings, ranging from dame schools to Eton... an educational free market... determined by parental choice and pocket.[8]

What these schoolings did have in common was that the overall quality was poor. Porter describes the public school culture as:

an initiation into the life of a gentleman: boys drank, gambled, rode, fought, and gained precocious bisexual experience.[9]

Most of the grammar schools, many with ancient foundations, had seen better days. Lord Kenyon pronounced in 1795:

Whoever will examine the state of the grammar schools in different parts of the kingdom will see to what a lamentable condition most of them are reduced.[10]

Middle-class demand for an education that combined elements of classical education with more practical subjects such as arithmetic was on the rise. In the words of Porter, this left the door open for:

hundreds of younger sons, beneficeless clergy and penurious writers to set up day schools and boarding schools, teaching anything from the alphabet to Classics, gunnery and navigation.... Their wives and sisters commonly acted as matrons.[11]

As Stewart experienced from the three schools he taught in, the quality varied enormously.

HAMMERSMITH

His first employer was Dr Bothie, who ran a small school in Hammersmith mainly for sons of the nobility. Dr Bothie clearly saw Stewart's potential, as he took him on without a reference. He encouraged him to continue his study of Latin and start teaching it, as well as learn Greek. Dr Bothie was a well-known scholar and editor of a literary magazine, the *Augustin Review*. He used Stewart to read aloud passages of books he was reviewing, which he then subjected to critical comment:

> *'Pass on, pass on, the fellow is a fool. Turn over a few pages, there, now read.' When I had gone a little way in this new place, he would again stop me, 'Ah! Read that again. Eh, why, the fellow has sense after all. Read on,' etc.*

Stewart learnt from Dr Bothie how to subject whatever he was reading to in-depth critical analysis, which meant that:

> *I was less than ever inclined to take all for gospel that was in print.... This I owe to Dr Bothie.*

EGHAM

After fourteen months with Dr Bothie, Baker alerted him to the fact that there was a vacancy at his school in Egham. The French master had resigned as well as the second Latin and Greek master. Wicks, the principal, wanted to combine both posts. Stewart applied and was appointed. He soon found why they had resigned. Wicks had been very ill for some time and seldom came to school. As a result, the school:

was in the most disorderly condition. The boys were complete masters of my predecessors and had driven them from the school. They began the same course with me.

Stewart discussed the situation with Baker and told him he was determined to take control, even if it meant using physical force. Independently of Stewart, Baker warned the class of what was in store if they misbehaved:

On learning this they formally banded together and determined to give it me. Numbers of them were great boys, several seventeen, and even eighteen, particularly two Portuguese. Hence I felt I need to be well prepared.

Next day I said to them when they came up in class 'Come, do you know your lessons?' They laughed in my face... and ran off to their seats in derisive cheering.... Next morning they were one and all greatly excited. I again called the first class. They came up keeping very close to each other. I said to them, 'Do you know your lessons?'

They all burst out in another derisive cheer. On this I immediately knocked two of the biggest flat on the floor, tripped up the heels of a third with my feet and was proceeding to strike another, when they all fled. Baker now interposed. Poor Wicks came in and said 'Come, come, we must have no more of this on either side.'

Later, according to Stewart, they became good friends and the ringleader gave him a present, with grateful thanks for saving him from a pattern of behaviour that would have led him to ruin.

ISLINGTON

On the death of Wicks, Stewart moved to Lemon's School in Islington where he taught geometry, together with French, Latin, Greek and English composition. Lemon, the headmaster, was so impressed with Stewart that he raised his annual salary from £50, which included board and lodging, to £80. Stewart worked hard on his accent, attending Thelwell's lectures on elocution, and, with Lemon's encouragement, spoke to all the boys in assemblies on various subjects.

On leaving the school to train for the Congregational Ministry, the school showed its regard and affection for him with a moving farewell in the playground attended by lots of parents, as well as boys and staff. The boys presented him with a number of books, which included Rollin's *Ancient History* in seven volumes and Simeon's *Skeletons of Sermons* in several volumes. In his address, Lemon paid this tribute:

> *Mr Stewart is a remarkable man. Whatever he does he does it with all his heart. This has distinguished all his teaching in my house and I have no doubt in future it will characterise his preaching.*

THIRST FOR LEARNING

Stewart's self-directed learning on the job had been strikingly effective. He now had a range of subjects he could teach, was a commanding presence in the classroom and, it seems, inspired many of the boys by communicating his own thirst for learning. This thirst went well beyond gathering the subject knowledge he needed for his classes. It involved understanding at a fundamental level the main branches of human knowledge. This required a highly disciplined work ethic:

I was now in the way of getting a few books which I felt I much needed. I got histories of England, Greece and Rome, with Robertson's History of Scotland, America, and Charles the V of Germany, and read them all. I now studied closer than ever. I rose every morning by five o'clock, summer and winter and never visited anywhere.

As an autodidact, Stewart's approach had the merits of improvisation, as he could follow his interests wherever they led, but it also produced the frustrations of a learner on his own:

I accidentally stumbled on Watts's Logic, one day, at a book stall. I had never heard of the book, and scarcely knew what was meant by Logic... this led me to get Locke also on 'The Human Understanding', Enfield's 'History of Philosophy', Edwards on the Will, Dugald Stewart on the Mind, etc. In this I got something that was quite to my taste – difficulties I found, but I never tired of the subject. I made many notes for enquiry, but I had no one who knew anything of the subject, to solve any of my doubts, or clear up my difficulties.

ENQUIRING INTO RELIGION

The most important area of enquiry for Stewart was religion. Does God exist? Is Christ the saviour of mankind? What happens after death? Stewart had been brought up as a Christian but had lost his Christianity in the prisons of France, latterly embracing the atheism of the French Enlightenment and Tom Paine. However, his experience since he walked out of the prison at Briançon had made him think again. Those who hadn't succumbed to the coarse brutality around them were generally Protestant men of God, in particular Methodists. Those in

Arras were *the most clean, orderly and well-behaved*, whilst the carpenter on the boat to Russia was *a pious, good man.*

For Stewart, the question of belief required both his heart and mind to come together. In his case, his heart came first whilst the struggle in his mind was longer and tougher. In Scotland, he maintained there was very little *in either heart or head* that disposed him towards religion, although he did concede that he was an occasional attender at independent or Burgher chapels.

By the time he got to Egham, he and Baker, who shared a bedroom and a sitting room, were *reading religious tracts, after we had gone to bed, with the candle on a small table between our beds.* Stewart claimed, unconvincingly in his case, that *we were both nearly as blind as moles, though there was some good feeling.* It appears that he wanted the Christian message to be true but, in his words, m*y head was still bewildered with the views of the French and English infidels.* There followed a long period of intellectual struggle:

> *Goaded by conscience and fretted by my connexions at Lemon's, I procured Leslie on Deism, then, Gregory's Letters, then, Chalmers' Evidences, then Paley's, then the Bishop of Llandaff's reply to Tom Paine and several other works on the same subjects. The study of these works, with the divine blessing, dislodged all my doubts, but the process lasted more than fifteen months, and it was an agonizing one.*

The next question was: which church should he join that best reflected his beliefs about Christianity? This involved frequent conversations with two of his fellow teachers at Lemon's and, once again, extensive reading. He was particularly influenced by Mosheim's *Church History* in the direction of Congregationalism. This sought to recapture the fellowship of the early Christians through insisting on autonomy for local churches in contrast to the centralised national churches of Scotland and England. The Church of England was an integral part of a political and religious settlement going back to 1662, which discriminated against the Nonconformists – a discrimination that was still on the statute book. The fact that Methodists were part of the Church of England until towards the end of the eighteenth century is likely to have ruled them out of Stewart's consideration. So it was that, in 1820, Alexander Stewart applied for admission to Hoxton Academy to undergo training to become a congregational minister.

TEN

TRAINING FOR THE MINISTRY

THE INTERVIEW

Entry to Hoxton Academy was not a positive experience; it was certainly not a welcoming process. Stewart had to submit a detailed application form, which included a summary of his religious views and his own scholastic knowledge, including which books he had read. He was then invited to appear before the College's committee when he would lead with a prayer, deliver a sermon and then answer their questions. He describes what happened next:

This was an ordeal at which my heart revolted at the time.... I attended at the time appointed. It was in the evening. I knocked at the door of the house, a servant opened and led me along a dark passage, opened a door, and put me into a dark room, where I had to grope about for a seat. Such a process was little calculated to soothe a heart already sufficiently palpitating with anxiety.

When I had been here about ten minutes the door opened again and somebody entered, and before I could well draw my breath I heard heavy sobbing, which continued until the door opened again, when I was called by my name. The name of my unsuccessful sobbing companion I never knew.

I was at once ushered into the Committee room. The president in a very unceremonious way asked me to engage in prayer. This over, he then asked me to deliver my address, which I did, though not without some choking of feeling and some incoherence of thought and expression. I was then asked a few questions, which, when answered, I was requested to withdraw.... I was again sent for, in a few minutes of time but many by the beating of my pulse. On entering the Committee room the chairman, Mr Thomas Wilson, congratulated me on being elected by the Committee. He wished me success. I bowed and retired.

MAKING THE MOST OF HOXTON

Following this unsettling experience, Stewart was quick to take full advantage of all the College had to offer. After years of teaching himself, he at last had tutors whose knowledge and interests he could draw on; after years of struggling to borrow or pay for books, he had an extensive library to make use of with his own separate study; after years of wrestling with problems on his own, he now had not only his tutors but his fellow students to converse with. These discussions started early at the breakfast table where they might have:

a little friendly conversation or sparring as the case might be.... This was a good nursery for conversational purposes – when and how best to introduce a subject; how to bear contradictions in the best spirit, how not to be too readily elated by applause. That breakfast school did me much good.

Stewart joined the Debating Society, where he relished the cut and thrust of reasoned argument and the advocacy of unpopular causes, such as abolishing capital punishment on the grounds that God is the giver of life and no one else has the right to take it away. By the end of his first year, he had become its president.

For questions relating to faith and personal belief, he and some of his colleagues met informally in pairs or threes in their studies:

> *to compare notes and seek Divine assistance. The Inspiration of the Scriptures and the Atonement were the most fully inquired into.*

Just as he had done in France, he made time for physical exercise. He and some of his fellow students used an enclosed space, what he called *a "big boys" playground*, for jumping, wrestling and other physical activities. On one occasion, they frightened a visiting deacon who saw them at play and:

> *raised his hands and eyes heavenward and exclaimed –*
> *'and these Ministers of the Gospel!!'*

THE TUTORS

At the age of thirty, Stewart was a mature student who, after all he had been through, was now experiencing at undergraduate level probably the best formal education in England. Albert Peel, Stewart's biographer, observed:

> *it is now generally recognised that for many years the best of the Nonconformist Academies provided a better education than was to be obtained in the Oxford and Cambridge of their day.*[12]

Hoxton College was, it seems, one of the best. He was taught by three tutors, each of whom had distinctive qualities and teaching styles, which were closely observed by Stewart.

Dr Harris taught Hebrew, Old Latin and Greek divinity as well as theological studies, which included the art and practice of preaching:

He was well up in the Hebrew, a candid critic on our sermons, a well-read Noncon. of the old school. He often produced deep emotions and even drew tears from many of us in many of his common prayers at the family altar.

Dr Burder taught mathematics, mental and moral philosophy and logic. Stewart found this the most challenging element of the course. The reading itself was demanding. Then followed the written essay, which the students had to read out before it was subjected to criticism by Dr Burder. According to Stewart, he had:

a clear but narrow mind, prim, stiff, and formal in all his intercourse with the students, always the gentleman but no less always the distant Tutor.

The third tutor, Mr Hooper, taught Latin and Greek. He was the students' favourite:

a genial man in all he did, plain in manners and dress, often very amusing in his teaching and explanation of the authors we read with him. He seemed as if he could mimic the tones of Demosthenes well, and at times he sang to us whole pages of Homer – he had a fine voice.

PREPARING TO PREACH

The students were well prepared for their most important function as a Nonconformist minister: to preach the gospel. Part of the work with Dr Harris involved preparing and delivering sermons, which were then criticised by the class and the tutor. Stewart called this:

> *sometimes a sharp ordeal, yet it was a salutary one; each man got his angular points rounded in his turn... How nicely it brings each one to his proper level!!*

On Thursday evenings, the students found where they had been assigned to preach on the Sunday:

> *from which many anecdotes were supplied at the breakfast table on Monday mornings... We met every kind of treatment when out on these occasions, from the gentlemanly to the opposite... when on one occasion I was at Leatherhead... a sudden death in the Sabbath School room prompted me to an extempore address of nearly an hour. Much was said of that address for some time after.*

By contrast, when he entered the vestry after his sermon at one church, the deacon accosted him with:

> *"the sermon!! well!! it may be very fine, but it's not the Gospel."*

CONFLICT WITH THE CHAIRMAN

Stewart embraced the role of student with enthusiasm. He also demonstrated some of those leadership qualities that emerged from his years of captivity in France. Notably, standing up to people who used their power to do what he considered to be the wrong thing. At Hoxton, the man of power was Thomas Wilson, the Chairman of the Committee that had elected him. Wilson was a key figure in the expansion of the congregational churches in the early nineteenth century. He had retired from business at the age of thirty-four to use his considerable wealth and influence to advance the cause.

In his history of Congregationalism, Albert Peel observed that:

In chapel building he was always to the fore, and dozens of chapels in London and in the country were built largely by means of his generosity.[13]

He also paid a particular interest in recruiting and training young men to become the ministers of these new chapels – hence his involvement in Hoxton Academy. Wilson expected to get his own way: he was not a man to cross.

Stewart did cross him. A dispute broke out between the Committee and some of the students. They had got into trouble for missing lectures to attend an ordination service, to which it seems they had been invited by one of the tutors. Stewart was not involved as he was standing in for an absent minister in Manningtree. The students who were involved asked him to mediate. In what he understood to be a private conversation with Wilson, he admitted that there were *occasional laxities and irregularities among the students*, whilst Wilson conceded that some of the Committee were *hard and overbearing.*

Wilson reported Stewart's comments to the Committee, which demanded that he provide evidence. Stewart refused to do so and when further challenged by the Committee, said in that case:

H. Room.   J. Cochran.

Yours truly

Thomas Wilson

9. Thomas Wilson

I must take the liberty to tell you also what the Chairman admitted to me.

Thanks to Stewart's stand, the details of his conversation with Wilson remained private. A compromise was reached over the original issue, but Stewart reflected on the aftermath:

From that day I long stood at zero in Wilson's esteem.

MALACCA, MOSCOW, MADAGASCAR, OR BARNET?

In fact, Wilson recognised that Stewart was far too valuable an asset to languish for too long at zero rating. He was an excellent student who had a positive impact on the student community; he was already becoming well respected in the nearby congregational churches, where he sometimes filled in for absent ministers or preached well-received sermons on Sundays. Moreover, despite his own very limited means, he paid his way through the three years at Hoxton without drawing on the support fund that Wilson administered. For eighteen months, he taught two afternoons a week at one of his old schools, Lemon's School in Islington, using the income both to pay Hoxton and support his mother in Scotland.

Along with his other commitments, Wilson was also involved with the London Missionary Society (LMS), which was very keen to recruit Stewart when his course ended in 1823. The first offer was to help set up an Anglo-Chinese College at Malacca. The object was to teach young Chinese and Malays their own and European literature *as subservient to missionary purposes.* Stewart eventually turned this down, yet he noted: *I was long harassed with doubts as to the decision I had made.*

The second offer via LMS was to work for a Russian nobleman in Moscow who wanted him to teach his children and spread the Christian message amongst the serfs on his estate, as part of the Evangelical wave promoted by Emperor Alexander. Stewart subsequently thanked God for *inclining me to decide as I had done*, which was not to accept. Shortly afterwards, Alexander died and was succeeded by his brother, Nicholas, who promptly ordered all missionaries to leave the country.

Stewart was clearly attracted by the prospect of missionary work overseas. Even after he had accepted the offer from Barnet, LMS asked him to take charge of the mission to Madagascar. Much later, in 1835, he was asked to take on the ministry of Hobart in Tasmania. He met the Committee of the Colonial Missionary Society several times before declining the offer, *as I could not tell what reception I might meet from the church.* Despite these various offers of far-flung missions, he chose to settle in Barnet and stay there. In the last resort, he may have had enough of foreign experiences and wanted to put down his roots in the London area where he had first taught himself to become a teacher and then trained to become a minister.

ELEVEN

THE NATIONAL CONTEXT

A NEW MORAL PURPOSE

To appreciate Alexander Stewart's ambitions and impact during his ministry in Barnet between 1823 and 1850, we need to look at the national context. Two developments stand out. First, this period saw the culmination of a religious revival that had affected a large part of the nation and transformed the fortunes of the Nonconformist churches. Second, it witnessed the end of fifty years of nearly uninterrupted Tory rule and a new lasting political settlement led by the Whigs with an important place for their supporters, the hitherto excluded Nonconformists.

The combination of a religious revival and a significant political shift injected a new moral purpose into the affairs of the nation and the conversations and actions of large numbers of its citizens. It was very different from the materialistic preoccupations of the long eighteenth century (the term given to the more natural historical period than the actual century. In our interpretation here, it runs from 1660 to 1830, which makes it a very long century!). This material focus on getting, making, and spending, albeit under a Protestant banner, was itself a reaction against the Puritan revolution of the mid-seventeenth century.

Alexander Stewart, of course, welcomed the return to the idea of the godly community. His ministry benefited from it, and he made his own distinctive contribution towards bringing it about.

RELIGIOUS REVIVAL

BRITANNIA RULES THE WAVES

Earlier, Stewart had witnessed the disintegration of the Napoleonic Empire from both sides of the Channel. After the battle of Waterloo in 1815, Britain and its empire had, in David Cannadine's words:

> *emerged victorious and triumphant as the strongest, richest and most powerful country in the world... by 1815 it seems likely that the total number of people living in the United Kingdom and the British Empire was approaching 200 million, or one fifth of the inhabitants of the globe... For the first time that proudly boastful claim, made in 1745, that Britannia ruled the waves, had serious and global substance to it.*[14]

Waterloo was the culmination of over a hundred years of global conflict with France with seven different wars fought, all resulting in British victories except for the massive loss of the American colonies in 1783. A highly effective collaboration between the landowners in Parliament (led by the nobility) and the commercial and banking classes had underpinned the success and ensured political stability, with the Hanoverian monarchy and the Church of England providing, in the main, compliant support.

There was no room in these arrangements for Stewart's predecessors, the Puritans. They were blamed by the landowning classes for the Civil War, the execution of Charles I and the subsequent political upheaval in the middle of the seventeenth century, even though the landed gentry had split more or less evenly in choosing to fight for king or parliament. John Morrill suggests around *4,000 on each side and perhaps 10,000 avoiding being labelled.*[15]

In the Restoration Settlement of the 1660s, the Puritans, now the Dissenters or Nonconformists, had in effect been excluded from the Church of England, prevented from taking up public office, denied access to Oxford University and not allowed to graduate from Cambridge University. Nonconformists could not legally be married in their own chapels, nor could they be buried in their own churchyards. Their numbers steadily declined in the first half of the eighteenth century and it seemed as if they might just wither away.

THE EVANGELICAL MOVEMENT TAKES OFF

That all changed with the dramatic spread of the Evangelical movement through the North Atlantic world in the second half of the eighteenth century. At its heart was each individual's conversion: the experience of moving from darkness to light through renouncing a sinful past and embracing Christ as personal saviour. What followed conversion were two commitments: first, to live a godly life based on the study and application of the Bible; second, to take the message of salvation to others. Enriching lives in the here and now would also save souls as the converted could anticipate an eternity of bliss as opposed to one of torment in hell.

The Evangelical movement in Britain took off in dramatic fashion with itinerant clergy such as John Wesley and George Whitefield preaching the message of salvation to huge open-air crowds often numbering 20,000, many of whom renounced sin and embraced Christ in scenes of high emotion. Wesley himself was an Anglican and wanted his movement, known as the Methodists, to remain within the Church of England. However, the Church of England, and its lay masters in Parliament, viewed religious emotion, particularly when attached to what they saw as the unbridled enthusiasm of the masses, as something very much to be avoided: a threat to social order and hierarchy. Ironically, it was often the local magistrates who left unpunished the mobs attacking the Methodist meetings and burning their meeting halls, incited both by the clergy preaching that the Church was in danger and the free ale that might follow in the nearby public house.

THE NONCONFORMIST CHURCHES RECOVER

The successors to the Puritans, especially the Congregationalists and the Baptists, provided a much more receptive home for Evangelical beliefs, whether these were formed in the emotional atmosphere of a mass meeting or, in the case of Alexander Stewart, as a result of months of study and reflection. The emphasis on saving lives and saving souls reactivated the old Puritan drive of the sixteenth and seventeenth centuries of spreading the gospel to the dark corners of the land. Only this time, as the British Empire had expanded through its successful wars against its imperial rival France, it had become the dark corners of the globe.

It was also becoming clear in the early nineteenth century that there was a huge Evangelical challenge at home with the onset of the Industrial Revolution and the rapid growth of urban populations beyond the reach of both church and chapel. The Nonconformists relished this challenge, both home and abroad, as chapel attendance accelerated in all the Evangelical Nonconformist churches. These now included the Methodists, who had separated from the Church of England in the 1790s. In 1851, the only religious census ever undertaken in Britain showed that half the nation did not attend church, and of the other half, nearly as many worshipped in Nonconformist chapels as Anglican parish churches.

THE EVANGELICALS COMBINE

What was also highly significant was the emergence of an Evangelical wing within the Church of England. According to Stewart J. Brown:

> By the 1790s there were perhaps 300-500 evangelical clergy in the Church of England, out of a total of about 10,000; they were a small but highly committed group. From the 1790's, these church evangelicals found influential support from a circle of wealthy lay supporters, based in the then-fashionable London suburb of Clapham.[16]

Their leader, William Wilberforce, was an Anglican Tory who voted against legislation that would have enabled Nonconformists to hold public office. However, he worked with them to advance the Evangelical agenda. Despite strong opposition from the Church of England hierarchy, the Evangelical wing joined with the Nonconformists, mainly Congregationalists, to form the London Missionary Society in 1795. That was followed by joint cooperation in forming the Bible Society in 1804, which had by 1814 printed and distributed through its branch societies over a million Bibles. Critically, Wilberforce worked closely with key figures from the Nonconformist churches to help achieve the herculean task of driving legislation through Parliament, first to abolish the slave trade in 1807 and then slavery itself in 1833.

10. Portrait of William Wilberforce, aged twenty-nine, by John Rising in 1790.

11. Barbarities in the West Indies.
A year after Rising's portrait, Wilberforce introduced a motion in Parliament to abolish the slave trade. This image by James Gillray shows a British overseer submerging a slave in a copper of boiling sugar juice because he was too ill to work. Nailed to the wall behind are the arm and ears of a slave. Wilberforce used this incident, amongst others, to denounce the slave trade. His motion was defeated by 163 votes to eighty-eight.

Wilberforce developed personal friendships with leading Nonconformist ministers such as the Congregationalist William Jay and the Baptist Robert Hall Jr. He sometimes attended their churches and listened to their gospel sermons in preference to the mediocre offerings of many of what he called "the formal preachers of the Establish'd Church." As John Coffey and Michael Morgan write of Wilberforce:

> *His ability to build networks that transcended denominational divisions was a critical factor in his success both as an abolitionist and as a religious leader.*[17]

We catch a glimpse of this indefatigable networking across the denominations in Stewart's diary towards the end of

Wilberforce's life (he died just before the act to abolish slavery was passed through Parliament in 1833):

The Bible Society was going on pretty well. The celebrated William Wilberforce took the chair at our third annual meeting, and it was his last public engagement. I helped him down the Hall stairs – into his carriage, He shook me by the hand – thanked me – I never saw him again.

A NEW POLITICAL SETTLEMENT

THE WHIGS TAKE OVER

The Whigs, who had become known as the party of opposition, finally took power in 1830. Impossible to predict at the time, particularly in the turbulent politics of the early 1830s, this marked the beginning of the Whig/Liberal ascendancy, which lasted, with breaks, roughly the same amount of time as the previous Tory domination – fifty years.

This was no mere transfer of power from one section of the aristocracy to the other. Within three years, against intense opposition of the Tory party and the Church of England, the Whigs and their allies, which included Nonconformists, Utilitarians and Radicals, had passed the Great Reform Bill through Parliament in 1832 and followed it up a year later with the act abolishing slavery in the British Empire. They had achieved this landmark legislation by embracing mass public participation in the political process through meetings and petitions presented to Parliament. It was, says Linda Colley,

arguably the only period in modern British history in which people power... played a prominent and pervasive role in effecting significant political change.[18]

12. *This print was published in 1831 when the Reform Bill was in the balance. Here, there is no doubt that the rotten tree, with its rotten branches, is coming down. A glorious future lies ahead on Constitution Hill.*

This was legislation on a grand scale: the Reform Act enfranchised sections of the middle class, whose ambition, patriotism, and moral commitment were seen by the Whigs as vital for Britain's continuing progress. The act to abolish slavery sought to prevent further appalling wrongs that had ruined the lives of millions of people and, in the process, blighted the reputation of the British Empire.

Taken together, this legislation signalled a radically new view of the role of the state. Hitherto, the tasks of central government had been, in David Cannadine's words,

essentially limited: to the raising of revenue by direct and indirect taxes and the prudent oversight of public finances; to the upholding of the law and the maintenance of order; and to the conduct of foreign policy and the defence of the realm.[19]

The new Whig administration believed the role of government was certainly this, but much more. It was also to take action on behalf of the people to create the conditions where the talents, energies and innate potential of human beings could be fully realised. Religion was fundamental to this vision of moral regeneration, as was education, regardless of whether it was provided by the Church of England and its parish schools or by the Nonconformists and their own schools and dissenting academies.

The Whigs had initiated a revolution in government in terms of its purpose. In terms of its legislation, through the Great Reform Bill they had perhaps averted a revolution in the country; they had certainly ensured that the landed classes would no longer have a virtual monopoly of political power. By abolishing slavery, they had taken on and defeated the powerful West Indies Interest and in so doing had laid the foundations for the moral mission of the British Empire. How did the Whigs get these measures through Parliament in the teeth of powerful, entrenched opposition and what does this story tell us (and would have told Alexander Stewart) about the state of the nation?

THE GREAT REFORM BILL BECOMES LAW

The new Whig government took office in November 1830. By March 1831, over 1,000 petitions demanding the widening of the franchise had been presented to Parliament. In response, the government put forward a bill that abolished rotten boroughs, ensured representation for the new industrial areas and gave the vote to many members of the urban middle class. This was narrowly defeated in the Commons. The Whigs resigned and the subsequent election was turned into what Jonathan Parry calls *a referendum* on the twin issues of parliamentary reform and the abolition of slavery.[20] The large Whig majority that resulted enabled the revised reform bill to get Commons approval, but in October 1831 the House of Lords rejected it by a majority of forty-one votes with, critically, twenty-one bishops voting against.

Rioting broke out across the country with the bishops of the Anglican Church singled out in particular as the villains of the piece. Stewart J. Brown tells the story:

During riots in Bristol on 29-31 October, a drunken mob looted and then burnt to the ground the bishop's palace and library, along with a number of other buildings... In Exeter, the bishop's palace had to be defended by yeomanry from a similar fate. On Guy Fawkes Day, effigies of Anglican bishops replaced effigies of the pope on many bonfires. Mobs attacked bishops in their carriages on the streets, or chalked threats on church walls.[21]

BRISTOL RIOTS: CHARGE OF THE DRAGOON GUARDS IN QUEEN SQUARE.

13. *This print shows the Bristol riots being crushed by the Dragoon Guards charging the mob in Queen Square.*

Despite the Commons majority and the threat of mass uprisings in parts of the country, the Lords continued to obstruct the passage of the Reform Bill. William IV, who had become king in 1830, refused to create additional peers to force it through; the Whig government resigned; the Duke of Wellington, the arch opponent of reform, failed to form a Tory government; the Whigs resumed office and, with the very real threat of popular insurrection, the Lords finally surrendered, prompting a catastrophising Wellington to declare less than a year later:

> *The revolution is made, that is to say, that power is transferred from one class of society, the gentlemen of England, professing the faith of the Church of England, to another class, the shopkeepers, being Dissenters from the Church, many of them Socinians (who denied the divinity of Christ), others atheists.*[22]

14. *The unchanging face of the Tory party 1828–32. Arthur Wellesley, 1st Duke of Wellington, Prime Minister 1828–30 and leader of the opposition to the landmark legislation extending the franchise and abolishing slavery.*

SLAVERY IS ABOLISHED

Alongside the popular pressure for voting reform, there was a highly effective mass campaign to abolish slavery in the British Empire. According to Jonathan Parry, abolition was:

The dominant over-all issue at the three elections of 1830-2.[23]

The Anti-Slavery Society had been formed in a meeting at the King's Head near the site of "Bow Bells" on 31st January 1823. Just over ten years later, its members had succeeded in their mission as the Abolition of Slavery Act passed through Parliament. They had taken on and defeated the West Indies Interest, described by Michael Taylor, its recent historian, as:

*one of the most fearsome lobbies ever known to British history... as these men corralled the national press, the City of London, and the Tory government of the day into the pro-slavery ranks, it became clear that the West India Interest did not simply have connections to the British establishment; it **was** the British establishment.*[24]

The Protestant belief that all human beings were equal before God and that therefore slavery was an abhorrent evil powered the abolitionist movement, which drew heavily on Evangelicals from the Church of England, the Methodists, the Congregationalists and the Baptists; it also derived much support from the non-Evangelical Nonconformists, especially the Quakers and the Unitarians, who had played a key role with Wilberforce in abolishing the slave trade in 1807.

The Anti-Slavery Society organised a formidable grass roots campaign of tracts, talks and petitions to Parliament. This was unparalleled in other European countries, where the abolitionist movement was limited to people drawn from the political and intellectual elite. At public meetings up and down the country, returning missionaries gave horrific accounts of the brutal treatment of slaves and the frequently unpunished violent attacks on themselves and their congregations. Women played a prominent role in the campaign. According to Linda Colley,

By 1830, there were ladies' anti-slavery societies in almost every British town.[25]

They organised meetings, raised money for the Society, knocked on doors to collect signatures for men's petitions to Parliament and submitted their own, one of which contained the signatures of half a million women.

At the height of the agitation over parliamentary reform in 1831, there were twice as many petitions about slavery as reform. After the Reform Bill became law, in the first election under the new franchise in December 1832, Nonconformist ministers urged their congregations, many of whom were voting for the first time, to support only candidates who had pledged to abolish slavery. Altogether it is reckoned between 140 and two hundred pledged candidates were returned. The Tories suffered a crushing defeat at the polls. Over 5,000 petitions with nearly 1,310,000 signatures were submitted to Parliament. In the face of the overwhelming majority in the Commons, supported by this mass popular pressure from outside, the House of Lords assented to abolition. They were, in the words of Michael Taylor,

still haunted by the events of the previous spring, when their intransigence over Reform, had caused widespread rioting.[26]

The West Indies Interest still had enough influence to insist on massive financial compensation for the slave owners, which was only finally paid off by the British taxpayer in 2015. Slavery in the early 1830s was still proving highly profitable, and the British economy was benefiting from it. In the end, the West Indies Interest, and indeed the establishment, had suffered an overwhelming defeat at the hands of a moral argument that had been advanced with passion by large numbers of the British people. As Stewart J. Brown concludes:

> *Slavery had been abolished largely because of a popular Christian and humanitarian crusade, led by evangelical Christians.*[27]

ALEXANDER STEWART

HIS EVANGELICAL BELIEFS

The religious revival, sparked off by the Evangelical movement, and the new political settlement set in motion by the Whigs, heavily influenced Alexander Stewart's life and work as a minister. Stewart was an Evangelical who was committed to spreading the gospel to the people of Barnet and beyond. As we have seen by now, he was convinced that providence was guiding the direction of his life: it was this that drove him and sustained him.

HIS POLITICAL LEANINGS

Stewart's account makes clear his political beliefs and leanings. As we have seen, these were probably first formed in Scotland and certainly reinforced by his experiences in France and his treatment back in England.

Stewart was in England for the last fifteen years of Tory rule before the Whigs came to power in 1830. During this time, he witnessed from his home in Islington, in 1819, the return of the orator Henry Hunt from Manchester after what became known as the Peterloo Massacre. Troops had charged a peaceful crowd gathered at St Peter's Field to hear Hunt speak in favour of annual parliaments and universal suffrage. Eleven were killed and many hundreds were injured. This was how Stewart responded:

> I never **leaned** to the Tory side of politics, but if I had, the conduct of the troops, during the riot in Manchester in 1819, and the subsequent conduct of the government, in reference to that bloody massacre, would not only have brought me **upright** but given me a strong leaning the other way. Hunt's triumphal entry to London, through Islington, on his return from that horrid affair, proved quite an era in my political life. I never saw a man more cordially carassed by the populace than Hunt was on that occasion.

By this time, Stewart was reading the radical William Cobbett's *Weekly Political Register*. We don't know, then, whether he was in favour of universal suffrage and annual parliaments, but in the early 1830s he was certainly a keen supporter of the Whig Reform Bill as a key measure in undermining aristocratic rule. Albert Peel summarises his diary entries at the time:

> Stewart rejoiced in the Reform Bill, and in some of the resulting reliefs to Dissenters. He went to Royston to vote, as his mother-in-law's executor, and was very indignant when Lord Grimstone, 'a very decided Tory', called to solicit his vote. He signed petitions against slavery, and against the Government's proposal to grant money for the building of new churches. (Stewart, in line with Nonconformist thinking, held that all churches should be completely independent of the government.)[28]

15. Peterloo Massacre (or Battle of Peterloo).
This print was published in 1819 by Richard Carlile who, altogether, spent nine years in prison for publishing radical tracts and refusing to pay fines. He dedicated the print to Henry Hunt 'and to the Female Reformers of Manchester and the adjacent towns who were exposed to and suffered from the wanton and serious attack made on them by that brutal armed force, the Manchester and Cheshire Yeomanry Cavalry.'

16. This painting by Sir George Hayter shows the first sitting of the reformed House of Commons in 1833. The location is St Stephen's Chapel, which was destroyed by fire a year later. Hayter undertook the work without a commission. He was an ardent supporter of parliamentary reform and wanted to capture this historic moment. It took him ten years to do so. There are 375 identifiable figures, each of whom sat for the painter.

HIS AFFINITY WITH THE WHIGS

The Whigs and Nonconformists were natural bedfellows. The Whigs supported civil liberties and opposed the legal discrimination against the Nonconformists. As Jonathan Parry points out, they also objected to:

> *the complacency, exclusiveness and inefficiency of the established church, the Church of England, and to its political bias as a bastion of toryism.*[29]

It was during a brief interlude in Tory rule, in 1806–7, that the Whig-dominated ministry under Fox brought about the abolition of the slave trade following concerted pressure, in and beyond Parliament, skilfully martialled by Wilberforce. Fox had championed the cause but did not live to see the bill pass into legislation in 1807.

Now, the Whigs were in power for more than a brief interlude and the character of their new leadership was much more in tune with their Nonconformist allies. In his youth, Charles James Fox had been, in the words of John Derry, a *compulsive gambler and womaniser*.[30] As a mature politician, he looked, according to Boyd Hilton, *dishevelled and unshaven*, as though he *had just come from his mistress*.[31] The new liberal Anglican Whig leaders of the 1830s were very different: sober, scholarly and serious-minded. They had, Richard Brent argues, revitalised the party through:

> *a reworking of Whig doctrine, nothing less than its transformation from the primarily constitutional concerns of Fox to an interest in the moral and educational welfare of the British nation.*[32]

THE CHANGING FACE OF THE WHIG PARTY

The Whig mission was to build a moral society, embracing Roman Catholics and Dissenters, as well as Anglicans, based on Christian values. This was a strikingly bold vision to unite the nation after three hundred years of bitter religious division. Much of it was music to the ears of Stewart. One gets the sense from his diary that he felt the tide of history, steered by God, was moving in the right direction, that the here and now was a good place to be, and that, with Christ by his side, he had much important work to do.

17. Charles James Fox, leader of the Whigs until his death in 1806.

18. Charles Grey, Whig Prime Minister 1830–4.

TWELVE

THE GRANITE ROCK

WHY BARNET?

In the 1820s, Barnet was a coaching town. It was the first stop out of London on the road to the north, where every day a hundred stagecoaches and a dozen mail coaches changed horses at the string of inns that lined the high street. This, Stewart realised,

> *did not supply a population on whom a favourable religious impression could be easily made. It was like cultivating a granite rock.*

Forty-six years earlier, in 1777, after a visit to the town, John Wesley had made the same point in the form of a question:

> *Will this poor barren wilderness at length blossom as the rose?*[33]

In the seventy years before Stewart, the Wood Street chapel had twice made special efforts to cultivate the granite rock. Both had failed. In 1758, Dr Thomas Marryat accepted the invitation of a small congregation to become its minister. According to Terence

Perry, the historian of Wood Street Congregational Church, this was an invitation that they soon regretted:

Not only did he appear in the pulpit in brightly coloured robes, but crowned his brief bizarre ministry by abandoning his wife and family and escaping to Edinburgh.... the church closed its doors and the building lay dilapidated for the next thirty years.[34]

The second attempt came through John Morison, who was minister from 1804–1822. He set up the first Sunday school but struggled to attract worshippers to the church. Perry comments:

For eighteen years John Morison worked very conscientiously with little reward, and few outward signs of success. In one church minute he notes sadly 'we are few in number' – and so they remained for many years.[35]

Morison resigned in 1822. Stewart was in his last year at Hoxton. Three members of the Wood Street congregation had heard him preach at nearby Whetstone. They asked the College if he could act as "a supply" for their church. He preached there on three successive Sundays, whereupon he was invited to become the minister on £100 a year and a house rent-free.

Stewart accepted the offer. Having preached at the church and met the congregation, he knew the extent of the challenge:

There I found the old chapel little better than a hovel, concealed from public view by surrounding objects, as if ashamed of its existence. There I found a few Christians so steeped in the spirit of helotism that they felt it their privilege to get 'leave of their betters to live.' There I found Dissent not only at a discount – hated by the church folks, suspected by the tradespeople, and fair game for the pelting of the rabble.

By now, Stewart was known and highly regarded on the circuit of Congregational churches with links to Hoxton Academy. He could have found a ministry with at least some signs of potential, so why did he take this on? We can only suppose that he saw Barnet in the light of everything he had endured and overcome since he ran away from home. Taking on "the church folks", winning over "the tradespeople" and facing down "the rabble" presented challenges he may have relished, confident that divine assistance in combination with his own talents would result in success. A more practical consideration may also have contributed to his decision. In his account, he says that *the place* (Barnet) *was high and healthy.* He had spent years in very unhealthy French prisons, notably the underground fortress of Bitche. He was planning to marry and have a family. Looking down on London from this perspective, Barnet would have seemed an attractive proposition.

THE TREBLE COURSE

Stewart accepted the Barnet ministry in March 1823. In October, all three of his tutors took part in his ordination service, which was apparently unprecedented. Clearly, they regarded him highly and Stewart suspected that their attendance was also a statement of their disapproval of Thomas Wilson's fall-out with him. As they took their place in the run-down chapel, they would have appreciated the scale of the challenge Stewart was taking on.

Had they reassembled in the new chapel ten years later, they would perhaps not have been surprised to find the building overflowing with worshippers. They might have raised an eyebrow on discovering that Stewart had also opened a school in 1826 and had just taken on students for a year's training programme for Hoxton and other academies. He was later to call this *a treble course* – the ministry, the school, and the students. This was a huge commitment on top of his own domestic circumstances. He had married Ann White in 1824 and by July 1833, they had had seven children.

So how was it that Stewart had ended up in 1833 on this treble course? Was it part of a grand vision or did it emerge under pressure of immediate circumstances and needs?

KEY DECISIONS

1824

1824 was a particularly eventful year for Stewart. On 13th January, he married Ann Kezia White, a member of his congregation. She was twenty-four and he was thirty-three. From the two accounts we have, it does not appear to have been a prolonged or elaborate courtship. First, Alexander Stewart, who recalled that in the chapel there were two family pews on either side of him:

Each of these pews was occupied by a family bearing the same name, though in no way related the one to the other. In each family there were seven daughters, several of whom were women grown. Of course I knew nothing of the topics of conversation in either family, nor of the feelings, if any, in particular; a veil must be cast over such things, and yet from one of the families something like a bait was presented me in the shape of some silver spoons with my initials on them. From the other family I got no spoons, but I got a wife. If you want any father particulars you had better apply to her for them.

The second account is taken from David Newton's biography of Halley Stewart. It is from Ann's mother who wrote a letter, enclosing a piece of bridal cake, to an old family friend shortly after the wedding:

> *Ann's partner... is a young Scotchman from Fife, of suitable age (a little older than Ann) and of agreeable person and manners, very intelligent and of good classical education – I trust also that altho' rather of an argumentative turn of mind, yet most decidedly pious, and most sincerely devoted to the cause and interest of the dear Redeemer. A very considerable revival has taken place at Barnet since his residence there, and we sincerely hope his gracious Master has yet much for him to do in that place.[36]*

Stewart now set about building a new chapel. He formed a committee from the growing congregation to draw up plans and raise the money:

> *Though we had not a wealthy man among us and but scant assistance beyond ourselves.*

Despite this, the plan was ambitious. It involved buying the two houses that concealed the chapel from public view, knocking them down along with the chapel, and in their place building a bigger chapel with open space in front of it and a new house resembling it to one side. Remarkably, the chapel was opened in October 1824. It had only a small debt attached, whilst the new house cost £400, borrowed at five per cent. In that house, Ann and Alexander's first child, Elizabeth, was born in November. According to Stewart:

> *Ma got through her first trouble quite as well as could be expected.*

1826

The new chapel was filling up, but Stewart was finding it a real challenge to get his congregation *to move out of the rut... of servility* and away from their obsession with *what would the Rector say?* Stewart was also looking hard at his financial situation. There were five mouths to feed in the new house: Alexander, Ann, Elizabeth (known as Lizzie), Isabella, who was Stewart's sister, and a servant. In addition, Ann was expecting another child. The chapel members, according to Stewart, had promised on his appointment to do all they could to advance his annual income of £100 *even to fourfold.* After the chapel had been paid for, the situation had changed:

> *I had no hope of any increase in income from the church for some time – they thought themselves justified in this course by the great efforts they had lately made in building the chapel.*

£100 a year was an inadequate income to support a married minister with a growing family. As a single teacher, Stewart had been paid £80 a year by Lemon. After a lot of thought, Stewart decided to open his own school for boys, day scholars and boarders, using the new building next to the chapel as the schoolhouse. This had remained unlet and to Stewart it made obvious sense to use it for a school – his school. He needed the income; looking ahead, this was how he could provide a first-class education for his children (at least his boys) when otherwise it would cost him money he could not afford; finally, he loved teaching. School teaching seemed to him to go hand in hand with his own preaching ministry.

1833

By 1833, the year slavery was abolished in the British Empire, there were no more helots in Wood Street chapel. It was full of Sunday worshippers, its various societies were thriving, and, under Stewart's leadership, Congregationalism was a force to be reckoned with in the town. His school was flourishing with *ten or twelve Boarders and rather more Day Scholars.* Ann and Alexander now had seven children.

19. Alexander Stewart

In an emergency, Stewart was asked to take on a young man and, for a fee of £40 for the year, prepare him for the training programme to become a Congregational minister. The arrangement worked well, satisfying everyone, including Stewart's old foe, Thomas Wilson. By now reconciled, Stewart agreed to Wilson's proposal that he took on a few students every year as boarders:

> *In this way I was supplied with students for a number of years, having sometimes as many as ten at a time. But the average number was about five. As our two houses were too small to accommodate these students as well as our boarders I acquired additional room from the house adjoining the school-house. Here I obtained, first two, then three, rooms, in one of which I taught the students separate from the boys.*

Thus, the treble course was established, initiating what Stewart called:

> *The most laborious – the most interesting and the most useful (period) in my life.*

Stewart was, in effect, creating a godly community based on one site, embracing the chapel, the schoolhouse and adjoining rooms, where schoolboys and students were taught, and the family home. The focus was on godly learning and living for all ages, from the cradle to the grave. Indeed, in 1834, the church acquired land at the pulpit end of the chapel where they built their own enclosed burial ground.

It was not uncommon for ministers to take on students to prepare them for the training programme; nor to set up their own schools. What was unusual, perhaps unique, here, was the triple nature of the enterprise, which, as we shall see, enabled Stewart to use the different elements to reinforce and strengthen each other. There is no evidence that Stewart was working towards this from the start. Rather, it emerged from his continuing need to provide for his growing family. However, he would have been quick to realise the potential of the treble course as a powerful tool in both raising his family and spreading the message of the gospel.

THIRTEEN

CULTIVATING THE GRANITE ROCK

TAKING ON THE RECTOR

Beyond the rebuilding of the chapel, Stewart's first major challenge was the rector of the local Anglican Church. Condescension and contempt characterised much of the Church of England's attitude towards the Nonconformists, whether in Barnet or Bengal. This is the Baptist William Carey's account of his courtesy visit to the Anglican minister in Bengal who:

> *received me with cool politeness… He carried himself as greatly my superior, and I left him without his having so much as asked me to take any refreshment, though he knew that I had walked five miles in the heat of the sun.*[37]

In Barnet, the rector and his successors demonstrated a similar attitude of superiority. He had just established a Church of England Sunday school and warned the arriviste Stewart against setting up a Congregational alternative:

> *Let the Dissenters beware of thrusting their sickle into our harvest.*

Stewart was having none of that. He called a public meeting to discuss the revival of the Congregational Sunday school that the previous minister, Morison, had opened in 1804. The rector put personal pressure on potential supporters, including Stewart's principal deacon, not to attend. The meeting went ahead, the school was opened with, according to Stewart, *a noble staff of teachers*, and soon it was flourishing.

Next, in 1826, the rector tried to stop the formation of a local ladies' branch of the Bible Society, which had the support of both the Nonconformists and the Evangelicals from the Church of England. He preached against it and had his sermon printed and circulated. He publicly attacked the Nonconformists and told his own parishioners not to attend. Stewart was a committed supporter of the Bible Society. He prepared his response to the rector in the form of two addresses to the townspeople: one justifying the Bible Society, the other defending dissent. The first was circulated on the day of meeting with the rector responding with handbills, personal visits and threats. The meeting went ahead. It was well-attended. Stewart spoke and the branch was set up.

The following day, it was announced that the rector had died. There was no inquest and no explanation. Stewart held back from distributing his second address in defence of Nonconformity. In some respects, he didn't need to distribute it. The rector was doing his work for him. In public, now on two occasions, Stewart had challenged him openly and successfully. In private, he was doing the same. He recorded a conversation he had with a Barnet lady who rebuked him for addressing the rector as an equal. He responded with a quotation from Christ in the New Testament: *One is your master and all ye are your brethren.*

Conflict continued with the new rector. The severe winter of 1829–30 caused much distress. Stewart set up a Sick-Poor Society to support those in poverty who were ill. The rector, in

Stewart's account, attempted to upstage the Congregationalists by hiring professional actors to perform in aid of the Anglican sponsorship of the same cause. Stewart condemned this as *personal gratification,* which left only *a contingency remnant for the poor.* His sermon on Christ's example of doing good was strongly attacked in the local Sunday newspaper, *The Despatch.* Stewart then distributed the printed edition of his sermon with a preface. On the same day, a leak, traced to a relative of the printer, enabled the paper to respond to Stewart with another highly critical piece. Stewart was not going to let his opponents have the last word in this very public spat. Albert Peel writes:

> *Stewart rejoined with Strictures, and the whole business raised his credit in the town, congratulations pouring in upon him.*[38]

What was happening in Barnet was perhaps an extreme example of what was going on in lots of different parts of the country where the Church of England's dominance was being directly challenged by the Nonconformists. The Anglican claim to be *the* Church of England was beginning to look somewhat threadbare in the face of what appeared to be the irresistible onward march of Nonconformity. The belligerent response of successive rectors of Barnet only hastened the march.

DEALING WITH "THE RABBLE"

Stewart seized all the opportunities Barnet offered to take the Evangelical message beyond the chapel doors. For many years he preached at Barnet Fair, which, according to *The Times* in 1834, was England's largest cattle market, showing up to 40,000 animals. The fair drew large crowds with horse racing and boxing among the many attractions. Stewart relished the challenge of open-air preaching to often rowdy, disruptive onlookers:

On one occasion, Mr Dinsdale who accompanied me, received very rough handling and personal injury while I got off unhurt with only the top of my hat beaten in.

Stewart always preached to the haymakers, many of whom came over from Ireland every summer. He preached wherever he found some space – in the street, the fields or barns lent by friendly farmers. This was a more receptive audience and he noted that:

I always felt peculiarly at home in such homely services.

In 1830, three of the Irish haymakers needed his protection from the rampaging mob. The bitter winter of 1829–30 was followed by a very wet summer, making it impossible to cut the hay:

Many of the poor creatures suffered greatly and made very urgent appeals in town for help.

One afternoon, Stewart was returning from nearby Whetstone with his four-year-old son, Alexander, when they came across a number of Irishmen fleeing from a mob armed with sticks and other weapons. Apparently, the Irish had stolen bread from some bakers' shops. Stewart got home with Alexander to find out that his wife and sister had gone out. He could see from his window the mob chasing three Irishmen down Wood Street:

I at once ran down to meet them without taking time to put on my coat or hat. I opened the gate and beckoned them to come in. I stood outside, and shut the Gate remonstrating with the various pursuers. Some called out,

knock him down – others, duck him in the pond. With
difficulty I got inside the gate. I threatened with a charge
of trespass the first who should force the gate. I pointedly
and by name addressed a constable by the name of Walsh
and said I would report him to the magistrates. At last I
heard someone call out – let us hear what he has to say. I
saw the tide was turning – took advantage of it – got on
the parapet wall inside the rails and addressed the crowd
for some time when they quietly dispersed. The three
Irishmen I kept in the chapel – gave them some food, and
when the night advanced they quietly left.

Stewart's reputation for 'muscular Christianity' can only have been enhanced when he took on Tom Dell, whom Albert Peel describes as *a retired jockey and Barnet's public house orator.*[39] Dell, fortified by gin from at least one of the ten public houses in the high street, had found his way into the gallery of the Congregational chapel, where there was going to be a lecture on astronomy. As the lights went down, Dell's oaths could be heard by all. Stewart ordered him to leave, which he did with a volley of threats and abuse:

The moment he was outside of the chapel I said to him
'Now, Sir, put your threats into execution. I am ready for
you' and began to pull off my coat. 'What', he exclaimed,
'A parson fight!!' 'Yes', I replied, 'and with the warrant of
Scripture.' He should like to hear it, he said. 'So you shall',
I said. 'Treat a fool according to his folly.' He walked off,
and we returned to hear the lecture.

WINNING OVER "THE TRADESPEOPLE"

The Congregational Church under Stewart was clearly a force to be reckoned with in the town. The Church of England parishioners would have been wary of him; the rowdier elements of the community may well have respected him. What did he do to attract people into his chapel and build such a large and loyal congregation in the barren wilderness of Wesley's description?

A FULL HOUSE

We know from the religious census of 1851 that there was seating accommodation for six hundred and standing room for fifty in the Wood Street chapel. One entry for Stewart's diary stated that:

> *The attendance at chapel so great that frequently some have to stand in the stairs especially in the evenings.*

Later on, he records that:

> *The attendance at chapel never flagged during these years – the church members gradually increased – the body of the chapel was filled with communicants.*

STEWART'S PREACHING

One reason for the full chapel was that its congregation had come to hear Stewart preach. In his account of the period between 1830 and 1850, George Kitson Clark noted that:

> *There was a great deal of preaching, indeed, among Dissenters, a minister largely lived by his voice.*[40]

Stewart's own voice was distinctive. He referred to *my half Scottish and half foreign accent*. He also noted that in the early days, he spoke too quickly. This may partly explain why his successor said in his tribute to Stewart that:

Few persons on first hearing him preach liked either his Matter or his Style; but when accustomed to the latter, none could fail to receive peculiar benefit from the peculiar tact he possessed of opening up the full meaning and design of any passage on which he might discourse.[41]

His obituary pointed out that:

As a preacher, he never aimed at the elaboration of sermons, but was careful beyond many to think them out well, and give the people something to think out for themselves.[42]

Stewart was highly regarded as a preacher and much in demand. He records that:

I was invited several times to preach at the Tabernacle and Tottenham Court chapel at the request of John Wilkes, Esq, M.P. for Sudbury.

This was the chapel associated with George Whitefield, the famous Evangelical preacher of the eighteenth century. On one occasion, he had to preach an early morning sermon, which meant staying overnight:

Ma went with me and we were accommodated at the Chapel House. The chapel was full, crowded to the door. It was an exciting scene and not easy to be forgotten. The text which I preached was "Behold the Lamb of God." Wilkes told me in the vestry after the sermon that I had given him the best view of the "Atonement" he had ever heard.

When the pastor was due to retire, the choice of successor was between Stewart, backed by Wilkes and other prominent members, and the outspoken, charismatic John Campbell. Much to the relief of the Barnet congregation, and quite probably the disappointment of Stewart, Campbell was chosen by a narrow majority. One much-needed outcome resulted: the Barnet deacons, alarmed by the prospect of losing Stewart, raised his annual stipend to £150.

Preachers in Victorian England wielded great influence. The most famous, like the Baptist Charles Haddon Spurgeon, acquired celebrity status. By the age of twenty, he had achieved what the Baptist historian Ernest Payne called *sensational popular success*.[43] Chapels were too small for him as he and his following moved first to Exeter Hall, then the Surrey Gardens Music Hall and finally the Metropolitan Tabernacle. This was built for him with seats for 3,600 and additional room for 1,000 more. From 1861–91, he preached there to capacity congregations.

Stewart was fascinated by the craft of preaching and its capacity, in the right hands, to influence people's lives for the good. Sermons were listened to and read, as many were printed. Dreaming occasionally of becoming what he called *a somebody*, he thought if that were to happen it would be through preaching. Mastering the craft would require dedication and time. His decision to open the school *put this phantom to flight*. Bidding a *sorrying farewell* to the idea, he determined instead to:

Preach as clearly, as energetically and as feelingly as I could.

These three adverbs, together with other clues, help us visualise Stewart in the pulpit. He would have conveyed an intellectual clarity and rigour about his exposition; a commanding physical presence and energy about his person; and a sense of joy and deep emotion about his conviction that Christ had come to save us all. His congregation would have been clear from Stewart's guidance both about how to lead their lives in the here and now, and, most probably, what they might hope for in the life to come.

We know how Stewart visualised the Christian afterlife from his account of the tragic deaths of three of his daughters, all under the age of twenty-one. After the death of Ann, just before her first birthday, he recorded:

> *I trust through God's mercy in Christ, she shall bid me welcome to a house new to me, but not to her.*[44]

Bella died aged twenty in 1852. Her health had been poor from birth:

> *And she had ever needed the most tender care both from her parents and all connected with her... She was a child of God and has now been long with Christ in paradise. May we all meet her there.*

Three years later, Christiana, or Kissie, as she was called, died aged fifteen. She, too, had been a sickly child. Stewart describes the situation just before she died:

> *In November I get a waterbed for Kissie who alas gets worse and worse. She evidently cannot be long with us. She dies on the 21st of this month. The scene in her room and around her bed some of us can never forget. Nor does one wish ever to forget it. My pen cannot describe it, but the scene is still vivid in memory. She felt she was going to Jesus – told us so – and we felt it too.*
>
> *A more sweet and lovable child I never knew, while she lived – more affecting death I cannot remember... what bliss it will be to meet that child in the immediate presence*

of the Saviour whose smile beamed in her countenance to her last breath.

We know that Stewart's sermons and addresses would have filled the minds of his congregation and probably stretched them too. His accounts of his daughters' deaths also point to a man of deep compassion who would have been sensitive to his listeners' emotions – from the joy of Christian fellowship and hope of paradise to the deep sadness and grief of loss.

THE GODLY COMMUNITY

Stewart's preaching conveyed the Christian message of salvation and what that meant for each individual in terms of how to live the godly life. Stewart's church enabled its congregation to live that life as members of a godly community. Like many Nonconformist churches of the time, it was an extraordinarily active enterprise where those involved could study and discuss the Bible, take part in philanthropic, charitable and missionary work, and become highly literate, well-informed and active citizens.

Ernest Payne describes what was happening in some of the larger Baptist churches in the towns and cities. One church in Liverpool had:

In addition to three Sunday schools and six Bible classes, a Savings Bank, a Women's Institute (with classes in reading, writing, arithmetic, sewing and singing for girls and women over fifteen years of age), a Clothing Society, a Dorcas Society, two Book Societies for the reading of essays and discussion, a Mutual Improvement Society for young men, a Mothers' Association and a Tract Visiting Society.[45]

On a much smaller scale, with far fewer resources to draw on, Stewart was doing something similar in Barnet, as his 1840 progress review indicates:

The Sabbath school continued to hold its head as high as ever – the band of teachers larger, united, and the annual meetings the talk and attraction of the town.

The Sick Poor and Tract Visiting Society steadily continued in the work of faith and the labour of love.

The Dorcas Society for some years seemed to bid fair to equal if not surpass the Sunday School in popular attraction. The monthly meetings were well attended. The annual meeting at our house often too numerous for our space.

Ma's Bible Society's cash receipts were regularly got ready every month and the annual meetings well attended.

The Infant School was taking a firm hold on the minds of parents all round.

Stewart ran the educational and instructional activities for the young men of the chapel and town. This included both the Bible Class and the evening class he set up for the Instruction of Young Men. This was designed to attract a wide audience beyond the chapel community. All he insisted on was that those who came passed on what they had learnt to someone else. Stewart lectured on a wide range of topics every Monday evening. It was so popular that it became absorbed into the Mechanics Institute when that was formed in Barnet as part of a nationwide movement to provide technical and scientific education for the working class. Stewart became vice president – instead of, he was pleased to point out, the rector – and continued to give lectures and talks.

David Bebbington makes the point that women played an essential role in the missionary and welfare activities of the Nonconformist churches:

Women, Bible in hand, did most of the district visiting on behalf of the chapels. They went into hospitals, infirmaries, workhouses, asylums and prisons: they cared for the needs of vagrants, navvies, soldiers, sailors and prostitutes. They organised sewing circles to make clothes for the poor and ran bazaars – in the nineteenth century an exclusively female venture – to raise money for missions at home and abroad.[46]

In Barnet, Stewart's sister, Isabella, was, in his words, *the moving spirit* of the flourishing Dorcas Society whose female membership provided the textiles that they made into clothes for the poor. The women of the chapel were most likely the driving force behind the Sick-Poor Society and the Visiting Tracts Society, which provided Bibles and religious pamphlets through house-to-house visitations. The Lady's Branch of the Bible Society for Hadley and Barnet supported the very substantial missionary movement overseas in which Stewart himself, as we have seen, was particularly interested.

This was a highly active community whose participants were engaged in improving themselves and the world they lived in. Alexander, Ann and Isabella made sure they thanked all those involved with annual tea parties, once the boarders had gone home for their Christmas holidays:

We began the year 1833 in much the same way, as for a few years past, by entertaining our several Societies at our house… they were anticipated with joy – full of life while they lasted and left abiding good impressions on the minds and hearts full.

First – the Sunday School Teachers – then the Tract Society – the Sick Poor Society – the Dorcas Society. This last was a very special one – all ladies and everything got up for the occasion in the best style.

For the first time, this year, we invited also to a plain Tea etc. the poor members of the church – the families, one evening – the males, another.

ALL KINDS OF LITERACY

In an age before compulsory education, the Sunday schools made sure that its children were able to read, using the Bible and its stories as the main medium of instruction. As we have seen, one of Stewart's first actions was to revive the Sunday school and thereafter he paid close attention to its work. He also did much to ensure that the adults of his church acquired a civic literacy by his very public engagement in some of the key issues of the day. We will look at three examples.

The first was a historic controversy within the Nonconformist community over baptism. This acquired a particular urgency after Ann gave birth to their first child. Like some of the others in the congregation, she had Baptist beliefs that insisted on only baptising those who showed true faith:

I devoted all the spare time I could command from pressing engagements to read up on both sides of the controversy and embodied the conclusions in 2 sermons preached as 3, from the length of the second, just before Elizabeth was baptised.

Stewart's research confirmed his belief in infant baptism whilst recognising that a plausible case could be made for the opposing view. The strength of his case won over the doubters, as did his call for charity and understanding on both sides.

The second issue involved a public conflict with his old adversary, the local Anglican church, over tithes. Tithes and church rates helped to finance the Anglican Church but eligible Dissenters, as well as Anglicans, had to pay them, much to their fury. This time, it was the rector of Shenley who issued a handbill in Barnet inviting a debate on the issue. Stewart accepted the challenge, but the rector prevaricated over the details of the debate; when Stewart challenged him, he withdrew, having been told that Stewart "had already killed one parson".

The final example comes from a bitter dispute mainly within the Nonconformist community over temperance or teetotalism. Alcohol in moderation had certainly helped Stewart at key moments in his years of captivity, whether it was surviving in the Alps or celebrating on seeing the sea at St Malo. For quite a period after Stewart took up the ministry, he made his own beer, having been shown how to do so by one of his female students whom he taught French. He had already formed a Temperance Society to advance the cause of moderation when what he called the teetotal "nuisance" or "mania" began. Their advocates launched a vicious personal attack on Stewart, accusing him of frequenting public houses. Some of his own friends and supporters joined the opposition in a very upsetting dispute, which he said gave him more trouble than anything else in Barnet.

The issue of alcohol divided Stewart's own congregation. Most likely there was unanimity or nearly so over the two great issues of the day: the Great Reform Bill and the abolition of slavery. We know that Wilberforce came to speak at the Barnet Bible Society and that Stewart was active in organising many anti-slavery petitions. It is also quite likely that he was one of the

Nonconformist ministers who urged their congregations to vote only for candidates who pledged to abolish slavery.

CONCLUSION

Stewart had created a tightly knit, godly community, which provided its members with a sense of purpose, the experience of belonging, and the prospect of progression in terms of knowledge, culture and material advancement. The particular attraction to the tradespeople, artisans and shopkeepers of Barnet was that they could gain the above whilst dispensing with the deference expected by the local gentry and clergy in the parish church. Stewart was quick to detect hypocrisy and snuff out any attempt to assert class-based superiority, as his masterly dissection of the Robarts family demonstrates:

> *They were bent on doing good, yet always selfish in the way of doing it... fond of doing good to the poor, yet ever demanding a curtsey from each, every time of meeting, whether on the stairs or elsewhere, the gardener to keep touching his hat as often as spoken to, even when in the midst of his work; professing Dissent, yet always giving Church people a right to preference; anxious to be considered a loving and united family by others, yet continually quarrelling with each other at home; concerned about the education of the poor, yet ever afraid lest they might know too much...*

> *They asked me often to preach on special texts, though I never once complied, that I remember. They had the impudence to ask me to call on them once a week and talk over with them the subjects I was going to preach on the following week.*

Elsewhere, Stewart records how:

*The harmonious workings of the Ladies Committee...
were marred by the aristocratic feelings of the Robarts
who could not brook the idea of acting in common with
the wives and daughters of tradespeople.*

FOURTEEN

PARENT AND TEACHER

As a boy, Stewart had enjoyed a rich and nurturing upbringing. On that fateful day when he walked out of his home at the age of fourteen, he unknowingly left all of that behind to struggle through adolescence and early manhood on his own, in an environment that was either hostile or completely indifferent. His survival made him determined that none of those young people he was responsible for in his various roles as father, minister and teacher would experience that feeling of abandonment and isolation. He made it clear to his children what he had sought to provide for them:

> *Such early training of mental faculties, moral feelings, social habits and religious sentiments as might, with God's blessing, turn out, in the long run, a much better inheritance than gold, patronage, or connexion.*

That is what he provided for all the young people in his charge within the context of that personal relationship based on love and care that he missed so painfully in the colliers and prisons of France. It should have been:

the golden period of human life when my early habits were to be formed and my moral education cast.

Instead, he was adrift and on his own, having:

to make my way as best as I could, often distressed to melancholy.

Settled in London, he made sure that, in the service of God, none of the young in his charge would be *distressed to melancholy*. Rather, they would be able to make the most of this *golden period of human life*, whether they were his own children, the scholars of his school, the students he was training for the ministry, or the young gardeners and apprentices of the town. According to his successor, he was always ready to:

counsel the perplexed, direct the enquiring and guide the young in the path of life.[47]

STEWART AND HIS CHILDREN

Stewart's diary provides a rich account of his family life, as well as of his work. It shows a father who took a keen interest in each of his children, how they were progressing and any setbacks they might be experiencing. Whilst he reported that their:

nursery history falls more properly within Ma's province than mine

he did much to stimulate their growth and, with Ann, provide that framework of love, care and wise instruction that they knew was all-important.

One of the first things he did as parent was to act on impulse and buy a carriage for his recently born as he passed through Drury Lane:

I had never seen anything of its kind before – as a picture it was a beautiful object, and the pleasure it seemed to promise to the possessor and his family was bewitching – the price!! – 6£ – that was a damper to my feelings, yet I bought it – and was not a little proud of it all my life long. It was an object of general attraction and admiration in the neighbourhood. In it you were all reared.

20. The godly community: chapel, school, and house at Wood Street, 1827. Lizzie is standing by the 'pram', with Alexander on the grass, as a schoolboy looks on.

Stewart went on to point out that in those days, there were no perambulators (or prams). Most nurses or mothers had to carry their children if they took them out. Now, Stewart's young children could see the world and begin to explore it through early talk. He was fascinated by the way their young minds were

developing. Despite all his work pressures, his study door –
sometimes, at least – remained open for his children. Here we
catch a glimpse of their first child, Lizzie:

> *Lizzie amused me one day in my study. There were two
> paper knives sticking out between the books on the shelf
> over my head – she asked for one of them – I gave her the
> larger of the two, which was by much the older of the 2.
> This she did not like, and asked for the other. I refused to
> give her the one she wanted – when she got into a little pet
> and went and stood sometime by the fire. In the course of
> a little time, recovering her temper, she comes to me as if
> nothing had happened, and asks if "I am not older than
> she" to which, of course, I said – yes, not suspecting what
> she was aiming at – when all at once she logically infers
> her question "then ought you not to have the larger one."*

The following vignettes highlight scenes in the early life of their
second child, Alexander:

> *Alexander, in a very peremptory tone, as if imitating
> me, calls to the boys, in front ground, from my old study
> window – "Go to bed children."*

Not long afterwards, Alexander saw some sheep going up the
street and found out that they were going to be killed:

> *He ran in great distress to Ma and asked if the boys were
> to be killed also.*

When Alexander was nine, his father told him:

> *a bit about my being in France... (he) was so excited that
> he could not sleep – he got up and came to my study and*

told me he could not go to sleep and wanted to remain in my study.

A year later, Stewart records:

while much confined to my study with a bad cold – Alexander comes – I much pleased with his conversation – speaking as it were to himself yet very evidently with the design that I should hear him – he brings out – "I know what I should like to be" – what, I said "with you in school if you think I would do" etc etc.

Stewart's next entry is:

Alexander writes a sermon on Mathew 11.27-29.

Stewart notes with pleasure when he gives the children presents: a book of pictures of three hundred animals for Lizzie and Scotch caps for the boys when he returns from visiting his family in Scotland. When they are older, he walks with them to London to visit the zoo or the National Gallery, or watch the soldiers being reviewed in the park or attend an anti-slavery meeting at Exeter House. When they misbehave, he responds without recourse to the rod or birch:

On Sab. afternoon get four of the children to my study – they have been doing something wrong in the chapel – went to prayer with them – they each write me a little note afterwards.

This was a very intense, Protestant, biblical upbringing. There was no rest on the Sabbath, as his son Philip's record shows:

7.00	*Prayer meeting*
8.00	*Breakfast*
9.00	*Sunday School Scripture Class*
9.30	*Morning Sunday School*
11.00 – 12.30	*Morning Service*
1.00	*Dinner*
2.30	*Afternoon Sunday School followed by walk*
5.00	*Tea*
6.30	*Evening Service*
8.00	*Singing in the home – with flute, violin, clarinet and bass viol (as used at the services).*[48]

It was an upbringing where deep emotions of belonging and separating were felt and shared, even amongst the very young children. On belonging, Stewart records a moment in 1833 when he *is laid aside with piles etc:*

Lizzie, Alexander, Philip and George in study – they read John 15 and sing – Philip leading – "that sweet story of old" etc. I dictate a prayer for each – Alexander came back and requests his prayer to be the same as Philip's as he liked it better. This was a happy meeting – not readily forgotten.

On the subject of final separation, two years earlier, Stewart recalls how the death of Ann, just before her first birthday, was shared with the other children:

Take Lizzie, Alexander and Philip to see Baby (who is laid in a double coffin in the chapel). Philip says – may I touch her – can she eat – can she see. They all kiss her – George also, but he was too young to know anything of the scene before him.

When they left the room Lizzie came to me in my study, and with a heart ready to break sobs out – Papa, I wish to die too – this was too much for my feelings. To divert her attention, I asked her to go and call Alexander. When he came I asked him if he wished to see our Baby again – Lizzie replied in an instant – we shall both see her again in heaven for a long – long – long time. She then asked me about a grave – a coffin – but my feelings could stand it no longer, so I diverted them from the subject.

THE SCHOLARS

We saw that Stewart had opened a school for day boys and boarders in 1827. He needed the additional income; he needed a good education for his sons at little cost; and he wanted to teach. He started with nine boys and by 1833 there were *twelve boarders and rather more Day Scholars*. To share his workload at a much-reduced cost, he began to use pupil teachers. The first was sixteen-year-old William Bevan, whose father paid Stewart a fee of £20 per annum rather than the boarding fee of £35. That worked well and others followed, enabling Stewart to record that *I never had a full out and out paid teacher*. Most of them did more than teach the scholars:

They helped me in keeping my accounts while Bevan and Jones wrote out many sermons from my Notes in their clear style.

When he started taking students for the ministry in 1833, he made sure they, too, made a substantial contribution to the school. In 1840, he records a few lines about its progress:

our numbers kept up – the boys generally did very well – our Examination and Recitation Days in chapel went off very well – the students taking often a very active part in getting the Boys ready. I was thus spared many an hour's labour in priming for the Recitations etc.

Philip wrote of his father as headmaster: *He gave and required the very best.*[49] Latin, French, Euclid, history, geography were all on the syllabus with books supplied by Cowings in the high street. The scholars had to know enough Greek to be able to read St John's Gospel. In addition, they had drill exercises, directed by ex-army sergeants, and singing and recitation classes.

Stewart was providing a first-class education within what we saw Roy Porter describe as *the educational free market determined by parental choice and pocket.* Standards in England, as we know from Stewart's own experience as a teacher, were very uneven. Most children did not receive any schooling. It was a key element in the Whig mission to put this right, using both the Anglican and Nonconformist churches as the providers. In 1833, Parliament provided an annual grant of £20,000 to provide part funding for the churches to build primary schools.

The Church of England, alarmed by its decline relative to Nonconformist growth, seized the opportunity, using the money to build a network of hundreds of Anglican schools. The Baptists and Congregationalists were torn over whether they should accept state funding. In the end, they decided to rely on their own efforts to raise funding, placing additional responsibilities on local churches and ministers such as Alexander Stewart. He became heavily involved in opening first an infant school and then a day school connected to the Wood Street chapel. There was, he wrote:

A strong current in the direction of Denominational Schools which had left scarcely one chapel of any note without a Day School. I could not bear the thought that we should be the exception.

THE STUDENTS

SKETCHES

In 1833, Stewart started taking students in on a year's programme to help prepare them for the Congregational ministry. This was right up his street. He relished the time he had with them and the opportunity it provided to prepare them thoroughly for the work ahead and build close relationships with young men inspired by the sense of mission. Many looked back fondly on their experience, often keeping in touch, coming back to visit and sometimes preach for him. Here are his thumbnail descriptions of four of them (one of whom did not keep in touch!) – Bevan, Beazley, Robinson and Sherley:

Bevan came to him as a scholar at the age of fifteen. As we have seen, only a year later, Stewart was employing him as his pupil teacher.

He became a decided Christian under my ministry – held frequent prayer-meetings with the boys – with my approval entered the ministry – came often from college to see us and sometimes to preach for me.

Later on, Bevan *obtained a charge in Liverpool, became Secretary of the Evangelical Alliance, was congratulated by Lord Brougham for his promising oratory at an Anti-Slavery meeting. He has lately had a church and congregation at Bow. Though our intercourse of late has been little, unbroken friendship has continued from the first.*[50]

Beazley came direct from the Iron Foundry in 1834. Stewart was a shrewd judge of character and was always looking to develop potential and open up possibilities from unlikely sources:

Mr Wilson paid for him as a probationer for Highbury (previously Hoxton where Stewart had studied). *He was a diamond in one – his natural talent was considerable – his application surprising. In most things he soon got ahead of those who had had a better early education…*

Though at first he was troubled with rather a low provincial accent, and a stranger to a large vocabulary of words, yet by sheer determination and industry, he became the best critic on the pronunciation of words at our regular readings at the breakfast and tea table. He willingly joined with the youngest class in the school and changed class only as he got ahead.

As he did with many others, Stewart continued to support Beazley beyond Barnet:

In due time he agreed to go to Van Dieman's in connexion with the Colonial Missionary Society. He was ordained at the Poultry Chapel – I gave the charge – Mr Wilson gave me 20£ for his fit out and I got 20£ in Barnet, chiefly from Mr Roberts. I got him his ship – he laboured honourably in Van Dieman's for many years and now he succeeds Mr Sherman at Blackheath.[51]

Robinson was very different from Beazley, though from a similar background and with similar potential:

He had but very little education – but very fair talents. He was not a favorite in our house nor most liked by the rest of the students. I had to battle often with the high Calvanism of some of the students, Mr Robinson clung to his to the last. There was some hitch that kept the Highbury Committee from receiving him – with some difficulty I got him to Cheshunt.[52]

Sherley had been with Stewart for eleven years, first as a scholar at the age of seven, then a pupil teacher and finally a student before he went to Cheshunt College. His father had been accused of forgery and Stewart had helped him escape to America: *his mother and his sisters always looked to me in my measure to supply his place.*

Sherley was a brilliant student. The resident tutor of Cheshunt College told Stewart that he was the only student they had ever received who could read a psalm or chapter in Hebrew. Sherley was determined to go to China as a missionary, but his health (and therefore the medical staff of the London Missionary Society) wouldn't allow it:

At last the fatal disease set in on him… consumption carried him off in the 22nd year of his age. I was much with him in his illness and often marvelled at his perfect resignation and thanked God for his bright dying hope, but I long felt his loss… I have preserved many of his

letters, not on the File, but in a small package tied round
with a bit of string, because I could not bear to burn them
with my own hands.[53]

THE PROGRAMME OF STUDY

Stewart taught both the boys and the students. This involved a
tight schedule and a flexible use of students:

From 9 to 11 I was always in school with the boys, from
11 to 1 I was with the students, and an hour to each in
the afternoon. I could very well hear all the students
could prepare for me in these three hours, and also the
more important of the boys' lessons in their three, with
occasional attendance and regular revision of what was
done by the boys under their teachers.

Stewart made sure that in their adjoining classrooms they didn't
operate in separate silos, but rather learnt from each other:

The students were not only at liberty to be with me in the
school while I heard the boys, but invited to attend, and
some of them even joined in the boys' classes at their own
request. The Students read Smart's Elocution and said
their recitations in turn with the boys in the classroom,
and all felt the more present the better.

The curriculum for the students drew on Stewart's experience
at Hoxton, supplemented by some of the reading and research
he carried out when training himself to be a teacher. It was
extraordinarily broad in its scope, covering philosophy, ethics,
classical languages and literature, science (which went under the
title of natural philosophy), mathematics, ancient and modern

history, constitutional law and biblical studies. Unlike Hoxton, where there were three tutors to cover the curriculum, Stewart taught all the subjects. He joined in debates and discussions *at the breakfast table and the tea table* and took part very competitively in the physical activities:

> *I walked with them, ran with them, jumped with them, wrestled with them, and took a most active part at our game of Fives... Browning was my most formidable opponent in wrestling and fencing: on one occasion, lest he should conquer, I roused up, put forth all my strength and threw him with such force that all feared for some days that he was seriously injured – all however passed off well.*

The programme had a strong community element where the students gained practical experience in preaching, teaching and other aspects of a minister's responsibility:

> *They occassionally preached for me, especially when I did not feel quite well. In the hay season, every Sunday, they went and addressed the men in every direction – were often sent for to supply Pulpits in the neighbourhood, while most of them took an interest in our Sunday school, Tract society and in my social meetings for prayer and exhortation in different houses in the town.*

This was of mutual benefit to the students and to Stewart, with his heavy workload and range of commitments. Making good use of what we might call his trainee ministers, Stewart was able to have more of an impact on Barnet and the surrounding area. In addition, they helped out both in the school and with Stewart's growing family:

The years in which most of you were born – in which you got your earliest impressions – these teachers and students – nursed you in your turns – played with you and taught you as you advanced.

The students benefited hugely from the intellectual challenge and the pastoral care that Stewart provided. In turn, he appreciated what they contributed to his children, his school and his ministry:

they gave a healthy tone to the boys in the school, increased our influence in the town, while, as critical hearers, to some extent, they had their influence on my own preaching.

FIFTEEN

AFTER BARNET

HANDS FULL

The treble course of ministry, school, and students was an extraordinarily demanding undertaking. It required huge amounts of effort, energy and resilience from Alexander Stewart, his wife, Ann, and his sister, Isabella. During the Barnet years, as the chart below shows, there was at least one new member of the family every two years.

Elizabeth (Lizzie)	November 25	1824
Alexander	May 25	1826
Philip	December 6	1827
George	July 24	1829
Ann	December 30	1830
Kezia	April 11	1832
Isabella	July 3	1833
Ebenezer (Ebe)	December 4	1834
Martha	May 13	1836
Halley	January 18	1838
John	June 24	1839
Christiana (Kissey)	July 30	1841
Josiah (Siah)	August 11	1843
Joseph (Joe)	January 26	1845

The imperative was to meet the material, educational and religious needs of the expanding family. The impossibility of doing all this on his ministerial stipend stimulated Stewart's entrepreneurial side: running a school and taking in students added to the family income, provided quality education for his sons, and generated additional manpower in spreading the Evangelical message.

We have already seen what the treble course required of Stewart: big commitments of time on several fronts. Building a large and loyal congregation on inhospitable soil, virtually from scratch, could itself have been a full-time occupation. In addition to this, Stewart was determined to spread the message of salvation beyond Barnet, and perhaps build his own profile in the wider Congregational community. He did this mainly through accepting offers to preach elsewhere. By 1837, he had indeed become sufficiently well-known to be included in the Deputation of Dissenters presented to Queen Victoria both on her accession and her coronation. For the accession, this involved wearing gowns, bands, knee breeches, silver buckles, silk stockings and then climbing the steps of the throne and kissing her right hand. For the coronation, it was the same outfit, but there was no kissing. It was explained that there were so many deputations that the queen found the kissing of so many hands *fatiguing*.

In addition to his work as minister, his weekdays during term time were fully occupied teaching the scholars and his students, with the boarders to look after in the evenings and weekends, along with all of his family responsibilities. On Sundays, he would preach at least one sermon, often two. Much of the Christmas holiday was taken up with tea parties for all the societies, leaving only the summer break as the chance to get away and recharge with friends or family.

It was perhaps this constant pressure that contributed to his own ill health. In 1832, he recorded that he began to suffer from constipation and flatulence, and then piles. The medical remedy was the application of leeches, six at a time, on three successive days. This lessened the pain but left him feeling weak. In an attempt to aid his recovery, he went with some friends on a walking tour of northern France, retracing the steps he was forced to take in 1805 on the first stage of his march in chains.

It turned out to be an eventful return, which must have triggered in Stewart all sorts of unanticipated memories: they were arrested by gendarmes and had to appear in court – ironically, he must have felt – for not having passports. After being presented as a priest, Stewart gave the court a short lecture in French on the priesthood and then apologised, on the mayor's advice, for not having passports. This was enough to secure their release. They returned to Dover and Stewart walked to Ramsgate where he met up with Ann and the children and they all enjoyed a cottage holiday by the sea. Yet, he had not fully recovered. Back in Barnet:

the straining at W.C. which in some degree still continued, with public speaking and general debility brought on a Rupture. I procured a truss and wore it for about a year.

If Stewart was under constant pressure, so were his wife and sister. Ann and Isabella were the human cogs that kept this machine functioning. After the birth of their fifth child in 1830, Stewart recognised that:

both Ma and my sister had their hands full, with only two servants to help them in the claims of the house and school – including the washing and brewing which were done at home.

On top of the very demanding routine in overcrowded accommodation came the unpredictable crises, brought on by the dangers of childbirth and the vulnerability of the very young to illness or accidents:

> *Elizabeth was on one occasion so ill for twenty four hours that we thought any hour might be her last... Philip fell out of bed before he was three months old and broke his collar bone, and when a little older swallowed a piece of the stem of a pipe about an inch and a half long. It passed through him... my sister informs me – George had eaten five worm lozenges. Doctor gives him an emetic – we afraid to go to bed.*

An entry for 1830 records the birth of their fifth child, Ann, at a time when the children had just recovered from measles and from *a nasty, virulent disease,* which ran through the whole house.

In 1835, Stewart records: *Ma up several times in the night with little Isabella.*

In 1836: *May 13/36. Born at 5.30 our ninth child and fifth daughter – Ma has suffered more than heretofore – doctor had to give her strong medicine – much exhausted when it was over.*

Then in 1840 came a hammer blow: the death of his sister, Isabella. She had a severe cold in January, then an acute pain in her side and then the diagnosis of the dreaded consumption. She died in August:

> *When the heat of the summer set in her perspiration became very trying. At last I mustered courage to tell her there was no hope of recovery. She put her feeble arms round my neck – held me for some time – kissed me again and again without saying a word – and I could not say one thing for a short time, rallying a little I said – are you sorry I have told you – she no – no – and again clung round my neck for some time. She after that talked very*

calmly of what awaited her – she had no troubles about the consequences of dying, but was not free from anxiety about the act of dying itself.

Isabella had come from Scotland to Barnet in 1825, at the age of eighteen, just after the birth of Ann and Alexander's first child. She had helped to bring up their first eleven children, as well as running the flourishing Dorcas Society. She had refused several offers of marriage. She had also told her brother, when he was considering the missionary offer in Van Diemen's Land, that she would not go with him. This may have made his decision, such was his respect for her and recognition of her vital role in the family. She was, Stewart wrote,

beloved of all that knew her... no wave ever seemed to agitate (her) – no breeze to move her from her course... Ma's loss and mine were inexpressible.

LEAVING BARNET

Stewart had recognised from the start the challenge of the treble course. He had gratefully welcomed the students from 1833 onwards:

not without misgivings as to the ability for the threefold task.

Seven years later, the death of Isabella prompted a radical rethink: how could he sustain the treble course without her presence? Did he want to? This rethink was accelerated by Thomas Wilson's own observations a year later that Stewart's hands were too full and the accommodation too small. Wilson suggested instead finding a bigger house in Barnet and giving up the school. He offered to provide a guaranteed stream of students, sufficient at the least to meet the funding gap. However, Wilson was ageing fast, and the London Missionary Society was looking to take on Stewart's role. Besides, and this appears to have been the decisive factor, if anything from the treble course had to go, it would not be the school.

Looking ahead, with his family growing up, Stewart was determined to continue with the school. But he increasingly recognised that it would have to be somewhere other than Barnet:

> *Few parents were disposed to send their sons, as Boarders, to such a school-house as ours, with its small school-room, small bedrooms, small playground, etc, etc.: indeed, it has often seemed to me, since I left Barnet, that it was a marvel that I ever got any respectable Boarders at all; whereas with a good house, in a good locality, with the lift which the teaching of the students had given me as a competent teacher, I might fairly calculate on doing well in a school.*

Barnet itself he saw as a place in decline:

> *The great coaching traffic was departing, in consequence of the new move for Railways, house property was declining in value, the population was decreasing, our church and congregation seemed to have reached their zenith, no probability remained that they could ever be improved, our family was increasing and our two houses inadequate to the needs of the school and the family.*

The needs of the family became even more pressing in the 1840s when their eldest child, Lizzie, was doing her very best to take on the role vacated by the death of Isabella:

Kissey, Siah and Joseph were born after the year 40 – all three required very much nursing care in their younger years. Kissey, like Bella, was always a very delicate child – she had to undergo a slight operation in the back of her head very soon after she was born... Siah early suffered from disease in his neck which kept him back in his education for years, and Joseph also suffered long with a bad foot.

The events leading up to Siah's birth in 1843 had been very difficult for Ann:

For some time before this confinement Ma had been much more poorly than heretofore. She had often to be carried from one room to another – on one occasion she crawled from one room to another when no help was at hand.

Stewart had decided early on in his deliberations that he and his family would need to leave Barnet. It took him nearly ten years before he finally severed all his commitments. Such were the ties of loyalty and friendship which he had built up with the Barnet congregation that he found it very difficult to talk openly about the way his mind was working. Then, finding a suitable, affordable place that had the potential to accommodate his family and a much larger school population was not easy.

Eventually in 1847, he took over the lease of Palmer House in Holloway Road from his old headmaster, Lemon. This turned out to be a fraught experience: Lemon was in financial difficulties after one of his sons ran up big gambling debts. It appears that Lemon deceived Stewart over the terms of the lease when he claimed that the schoolroom was not included. Rather than incur the risks and costs of court action, Stewart paid him £80. This soured what had been a strong relationship based on mutual respect, though Stewart put the blame on his son, never forgetting *what Lemon was when the sun shone on his path.*

Barnet Congregational Church and Alexander Stewart still needed each other. Stewart was not taking on another ministry. He thought that the headship of a larger school would be sufficient in terms of income and workload after the challenges of the treble course. The chapel authorities in Barnet knew how difficult it would be to find anyone as gifted as Stewart to take his place. They wanted to hang on to whatever they could. Meanwhile, Stewart had no income from the new school apart from a few of the boys who transferred from Barnet. It all had to start virtually from scratch with no guarantee of success. In addition, there were significant costs for furnishing and conversion work that were needed at Palmer House.

RESIGNATION AND RETURN

The result was that Stewart resigned from the ministry and then promptly accepted the chapel's unanimous invitation to become its pastor on specified terms and conditions. These included Stewart's commitment to preach twice on Sunday and once in the week, and to attend funerals, baptisms and public meetings. He was free to reside in Barnet or elsewhere; his income was to come from pew rents, not the annual stipend; all the societies were to manage themselves.

Ideally, the whole family would have moved together to their new and much larger surroundings. Stewart records the excitement when they first visited Palmer House, described by Halley Stewart's biographer, David Newton, as:

a palatial place compared with the manse and, at the time it was built, the last house between Holloway and Highgate. The main part of this substantial building had a stately bow front. Three storey wings flanked it on both sides.[54]

I shall not attempt, Stewart wrote, *to give you any idea of the feeling which ran through our family circle when it was known that we had taken such a large house, and in London. All seemed to feel as if lifted into a higher region – into a new grade in society.*

With responsibilities still in Barnet, the family had to separate into *two spheres of labour* with Lizzie, Alexander and George managing Palmer House; Ann, Philip and the younger children at Wood Street (where the school continued); and Stewart residing at both. The arrangement worked on a pragmatic level. The pew rents brought in as much as his annual stipend of £150, whilst he also relied on the generosity and support of his Barnet friends and congregation:

I could not have done but through the assistance I got through old Barnet friends giving me credit from half year to half year, which I could not have secured in a new sphere where I was unknown. We long had all our grocery – all our meat and most of our drapery etc from Barnet. In this way, with the income I got from the chapel, we were able to keep our heads above water from 47 to the closing month of 50, when I finally left Barnet.

RELIGIOUS CENSUS

Three months after he finally left Barnet, on Sunday 31st March 1851, Britain's only religious census was conducted. It showed that Stewart's packed chapel with people standing was a thing of the past. The census form records there was sitting accommodation for six hundred with standing room for fifty. On that particular Sunday, 299 attended in the morning and 171 in the evening. The average for the previous year was stated as 250 in the morning and two hundred in the evening. In the remarks column on the form, the Deacon recorded that:

> *the minister who has had the charge of the Church has left and his successor has not yet entered on the Charge. The retiring minister has been pastor of the Church for 27 years.*[55]

Stewart would have been annoyed to find that the nearby Anglican Church of St John the Baptist had more worshippers (379 in the morning and 258 in the evening). Even so, in terms of its own capacity, it was just over half full for the morning worship. Perhaps this mirrored a decline in Barnet's fortunes or the tenacity of the granite rock. Perhaps the decline in Congregational attendance showed the difficulty facing the sixty-one-year-old Stewart as he commuted between Islington and Barnet, with inevitably many of his thoughts focusing on the future. Whatever the explanation, the situation was a sharp reminder of the particular importance in Nonconformity of the character and presence of the minister and the demands of his office.

PREACHING AND TEACHING

Once he had left Barnet, Stewart was able to concentrate on those aspects of his work that he loved most: preaching and teaching. As a preacher, he remained much in demand in some very influential centres of dissent:

> *I preached frequently at places in the neighbourhood – at Union Chapel – Tabernacle and Tottenhamcourt*

Road – Paddington chapel – for Dr.Price, Baptist, &
Howard Minton & Baptist Noel – S. Martin's – Dr Reid's
– Binney's – The Poultry – Clairmont – The City Road
– the Scotch Church in Holloway Road – Morris' at the
corner of Caledonian and Camden Road – Bedford new
town chapel when my friend Rogers settled there, and
afterwards.

In fact, there were too many demands for his services in the pulpit. His old friend, Dr Bennet, put his finger on the problem:

I (Stewart) *told him how I felt in respect to such numerous calls, with the claims of my school. On this, the good Doctor, in his characteristic style said "What, Mr Stewart – have you lived so long and taught so much and have not learnt to say – no."*

The school did need by far the most of his attention. He had to build up the numbers quickly at a particularly demanding time, before his eldest sons were settled in their own careers, with lots of young children still to support. By 1853, any thoughts that he might have had of at least one of his sons partnering him at Palmer House were up in the air. Alexander, George and Philip had left home and Ebe had gone into business. Philip, who had been teaching first at Barnet and then at Palmer House, had left to set up his own school in Braintree. Despite all this, in the same year, the indefatigable Stewart was able to report that:

By midsummer the school began to look up – a fact which cheers my mind more than the sight of land after a struggling and doubtful voyage. Our Prize Day went off well and Dr Campbell (by now a parent of three boys at the school) gave a full account of it in the British Banner.

He gave a similar account of succeeding Prize Days for a
number of years, which did the school great service.

Numbers continued to grow, many coming from abroad –
particularly Guernsey and France – reaching a peak in 1857
when Stewart recorded ninety-nine boys on the roll, seventy
boarders and twenty-nine day scholars.

I longed to have the hundredth but he never came.

Thereafter, the typical annual entry reads as it did for 1861:

The school not what it has been and yet it is good.

By 1856, three of his sons (Alexander, Philip and John) were on
the Palmer House payroll and contributing to the school. Philip's
school in Braintree had not been a success and he returned to
Palmer House. He was the only son still working there in 1861,
when at a family meeting it was agreed that he would run the
school as resident manager, whilst his father would move to 408
Camden Road but continue teaching at Palmer House. Nothing
was written down. Philip interpreted the financial arrangements
differently from his father. This generated some ill-feeling but
by 1864, Stewart is recording that they have negotiated a new
arrangement:

Philip and I sign the new agreement about Palmer House,
to which Ebe puts his name also. I retain the document.

They had clearly learnt their lesson.

21. Three of Alexander's eight sons:
Ebenezer (Ebe), Josiah (Siah) and Joseph (Joe) c.1860.

Stewart finished recording in his diary in 1869, when he was seventy-nine. The entries over the previous two years show him actively involved in family affairs and social events, keeping up with old friends, retaining a keen interest in scientific research and topical debate, and still contributing to the school.

With regard to the school, he continues to teach French and is lecturing on physical geography. He begins *the delivery of my revised lectures on astronomy at P.H.* (Palmer House). In the same year, 1869, he attends the anniversary meeting of the Barnet Sunday school, taking a cab with three of his children. One of his old friends recalls his first sermon at Barnet, whilst on another occasion, he meets with his former deacon from Barnet and they have a conversation on Darwinism. A year earlier, in September, he goes with Lizzie and her seventy-year-old husband, the admiral, to Eastbourne. They take a boat to Hastings and before long are in serious difficulties:

> *The wind and sea rise – after being out for four hours, and far off land, the wind and sea still rising – the boatman doubting if it were not too rough to land at Hastings.*

They turn back, eventually getting to dry land, with the admiral declaring, "*I never in my life felt more thankful for a safe landing.*" This was a few miles from Brighton near where Stewart had been first of all shipwrecked and later captured by the French over sixty years ago. We can only imagine what was going through his mind.

During this period, he is writing up the story of the earlier stages of his life in ink and noting in his diary that he is *specially interested in reading the autobiography of Gladstone.* He goes to a dog show with Lizzie and travels to Newcastle by steamer to stay with his son, George, and attend the chapel where he is preaching. His views on alcohol appear not to have changed:

Alexander sends me 1 dozen of whisky, and Ma 1 dozen of ginger wine.

Nor have his old skills deserted him, as one of his last entries indicates:

22. *Alexander Stewart smoking a pipe.*

Oct 11 – Baptise Phillip's Marion at P.H. – large company – my address on this occasion seems to have been specially acceptable – it was extempore – I have since penned down the leading thoughts.

His final entry on 31st December 1869 reads:

Ebe, Siah and Joe come home very late from their party – about four in the morning.

Shortly afterwards, he and Ann retired to Branbridges in Kent where they celebrated their golden wedding in 1874. Alexander died on the 3rd of November that year. His obituary recorded that:

23. Ann and Alexander in their later years

In his last illness his mind remained unclouded to the end.
He was calm and hopeful, but not ecstatic.[56]

Ann died six months later on 5th April 1875. They are both buried in the family plot at Abney Park Cemetery, Stoke Newington. Alexander's funeral was conducted by two of the men he had helped to prepare for the ministry: Revd Beazley, who had come from the Iron Foundry with a "low provincial accent", and Dr Allon, twice Secretary of the Congregational Union.

The inscription on the stone reads:

Erected by eight sons and three surviving daughters to the
memory of the REV. ALEXANDER STEWART Minister of the
Congregational Church Barnet
1825 to 1853
Born 29 May 1790 Died 3 November 1874

"Thou shalt come to thy grave of full age like as a shock of corn
cometh in his season."

"Children's children are the crown of old men and the glory of
their children is their father."

Ann Kezia wife of the above born 2 May 1799 died 5 April 1875
Ann second daughter died 24 November 1831 aged 11 months
Isabella fourth daughter died 20 December 1853 aged 20 years
And Christiana sixth daughter died 21 November 1856 aged 15 years

24. Memorial gravestone of Alexander Stewart at Abney Park Cemetery.

SIXTEEN

SURVIVAL, REVIVAL AND MORAL REVOLUTION

FAMILY CONNECTION

My telling of this story is the result of a book and a portrait. The book was *The Life of Alexander Stewart*, written by himself to 1815 and abridged by Dr Albert Peel to 1874. It was first published in 1947 and intended for private circulation within the Stewart family, which is how I got my copy. The inscription inside reads:

> *John Stewart Williams* (my father)
> *from*
> *His Mother, Marjorie*
> *Daughter of Josiah Stewart*
> *Grand daughter of Alexander Stewart.*
> *Christmas 1950*   *"Morlands"*

The portrait was of Alexander Stewart (see page 94). It was passed on to me by my grandmother and hangs in our front room.

25. Marjorie Stewart, granddaughter of Alexander, at her wedding to Harold Williams in 1906.

26. Marjorie (née Stewart) and Harold Williams and their family, at Morlands in Croydon, 1950. Marjorie is seated second from right. Her eldest son, John, is standing far right. The author is sitting on the grass without a tie; his cousin, Ros, is sitting, second child on the right.

As a student and teacher of history, who is related to Alexander Stewart, I would have no excuse for not writing this book. As you will have realised, it is an extraordinary story, but it was only when I delved into it that I realised that his story revealed another extraordinary story: that of how the descendants of the Puritans, the Evangelical Nonconformists, returned from the margins of British society to make a significant contribution towards the transformation of the moral landscape of the nation. So this has become a tale of two stories, connected and illuminated by Stewart's own example of moral fortitude and learnt godliness.

THE STORY OF ALEXANDER STEWART

We must forever be grateful that Stewart decided to write down for the benefit of his children an account of his early life. It reads like a nineteenth-century version of *Pilgrim's Progress*, in which he overcomes all manner of adversity through the guiding hand of providence. In Stewart's story he has deserted God, but God has not deserted him. Once he had passed the test, it was God's guiding hand that steered him to safety and remained by his side as he dedicated his life to the service of God through ministering unto others.

We have to remind ourselves that the first part of this story, when he came near to death on at least seventeen occasions, is true! It is not the creation of a literary dissenter like Bunyan. The BBC did remember and share that fact in 1958, when they broadcast a schools' radio programme on Alexander Stewart as part of a series of exemplary characters whose lives told the story of British history. This is a remarkable story of survival, but one which, despite the best efforts of the BBC, is not well known.[57]

HIS LEADERSHIP ATTRIBUTES

The attributes Stewart demonstrated in ensuring his survival were broadly those that enabled him to flourish during his time in London and the twenty-seven-year period of his Barnet ministry that followed. Any good contemporary book on leadership would highlight those four qualities we identified in Chapter 8: a moral compass, curiosity, resilience, and emotional intelligence.

Just as he stood up to the bullies on the boats and in the prisons, so did he challenge what he saw as any abuse of power, whether it came from the treasurer of Hoxton College, the rector of Barnet or the mob at the gate. His intellectual curiosity took him, and those he taught, from the shores of the ancient civilisations to the contemporary world of science – whether it be navigation, astronomy or evolution. His resilience enabled him to persevere with the extraordinarily demanding treble course of ministry, scholars, and trainee students, whilst being an active parent of fourteen children. Through his emotional intelligence, he built those relationships with his congregation, his family and those he taught, which underpinned his success.

HIS SOCIAL MOTIVES

What made Alexander Stewart tick? What energised him and gave him a buzz, shaping behaviours that satisfied those sources of energy? In his book *Human Motivation*, David McClelland identified the three social motives that have a strong influence on how we behave: achievement, which we satisfy by either outperforming others and/or exceeding our personal best; power, which is either socialised, where we derive satisfaction from empowering others, or personalised, where we use our power to control others; and affiliation, which we satisfy by maintaining warm personal relations with others.[58]

We each have our own motive profile, which can be accurately assessed by writing a set of stories about open-ended pictures, such as a couple sitting on a park bench. Whilst we can't do that with Stewart, there are plenty of clues from his writings about what did energise him. We can use these to suggest that his own motivational profile would most likely have been high on achievement and socialised power, and low on affiliation.

Stewart was very competitive. We saw it in the barracks at Sarrelibre, where, egged on by the inmates, he was competing with a rival for apples in running and wrestling competitions. In Barnet, he was determined to beat his student, Browning, at wrestling and fencing, even at the risk (which materialised) of injury to Browning. Beyond the games, he was competing with the different rectors and curates of Barnet throughout his tenure there and he relished it. He proudly recorded that he, not the rector, had been asked to be vice president of the Mechanics' Institute. As well as competing with others, his own achievement metrics were very important to him, whether it was a full congregation or a hundred pupils on roll.

However, as the authors of *Leadership Run Amok: the Destructive Potential of Overachievers* point out:

> *In the short term, through sheer drive and determination, overachieving leaders may be very successful, but there's a dark side to the achievement motive.... Overachievers tend to command and coerce, rather than coach and collaborate, thus stifling subordinates.*[59]

In their 1990s study of 2,000 IBM managers, the researchers found that the most effective group demonstrated a strong drive to achieve but worked through others, using coaching to create strong teams. The focus was not so much on "I" but "us".[60] We can see Stewart doing the same in Barnet, achieving the godly community through highly effective teams of the trainee ministers, the Sunday school teachers, the Bible Society and the Dorcas Society.

This makes it likely that alongside a high achievement drive, he was also energised by socialised power, where empowering others gave him real satisfaction. This was very much in evidence when he enabled the young men he was training to take the next step forward in their life of service to God, especially those from disadvantaged or unlikely backgrounds. Here he talks about Nisbet:

Nisbet was at first a Day Scholar – his father was a butcher in Barnet, his mother a member of our Church. I found he had promising talent and took an interest in him, induced his father to leave him longer at school than he intended or indeed could afford… At last indeed his father declined to pay anything at all. I then took him entirely at my own cost.

Like Bevan he became a Christian under my ministry – wished to enter the ministry which I encouraged, but could not send him to College for want of pecuniary means. He continued to teach and I to instruct him for two or three years, when an opening for his services in Van Dieman's land presented itself, and was accepted by him. I got Mr. Thomas Wilson to pay his passage, and managed to get him a good fit out in Barnet… I got him a ship and he left for Van Dieman's in the year '35 where he has been ever since. Thence he wrote me many long letters.[61]

With regard to the remaining social motive, affiliation, leaders with a high affiliative drive get satisfaction from being on warm personal terms with others. They often find it challenging to have difficult conversations and tend to avoid them or not handle them well. Stewart could not have survived in France in the way he did, nor prospered in Barnet, without having difficult conversations. He was skilled at it and, it seems, rather relished the opportunity when he saw that it was needed. His likely motivational profile, of high achievement, high socialised power and low affiliation, coupled with his leadership attributes, go a long way to explaining his impact and effectiveness.

HIS PROTESTANT FAITH

Fuelling his work ethic and drive to succeed was his Evangelical Protestant faith, with its twin demand to live the gospel and spread the message. Unusually, it had three dimensions: intellect, emotion, and muscle. His Christianity was deeply intellectual – it took him more than fifteen months of study before he was convinced of the truth of the Christian message and the denomination to which he would belong. It was also rooted in emotion and a sense of the possibilities of life on earth, undoubtedly sharpened by the loss of his youth in the prisons of France. His was a Christianity of heart as well as head, of imagination as well as analysis. Finally, as Tom Dell would have testified, it was muscular, when it needed to be. He drew on all three elements, unlike the public school successors to Thomas Arnold, whose narrow version of 'muscular Christianity' elbowed out the combination of passionate intensity and intellectual rigour demonstrated by Arnold and his contemporaries.

WARTS AND ALL?

At this point, we might ask: is this all too good to be true? Does Stewart have no weaknesses or failings? Readers will bear in mind that this account is written by one of his descendants, who is in sympathy with what he stood for and proud of the way he lived his life. Moreover, his account is largely based on Stewart's own account. As a high achiever, Stewart might have been tempted to gloss over any shortcomings. Certainly, it would have been good to have had independent contemporary views of Stewart, both from those close to him, such as his ministerial trainees, and his Protestant rivals in the Anglican Church at the end of Wood Street.

Frustratingly, Stewart burnt much of his correspondence, whilst the contemporary Anglican record, as outlined in Adrian Esdaile's recent account of St John the Baptist Church in Barnet, concentrates on the challenges faced by the building of the new church passage, not those presented by the incumbent of Wood Street Congregational Church.[62]

We do have his mother-in-law's comment that Stewart was *somewhat of an argumentative turn of mind*. Maybe in his position of authority he was too used to getting his own way; or perhaps he said what he thought, and she didn't like it. We can't draw any conclusions on such a scrap, intriguing though it is. Stewart's own account points to his love of debate and reasoned argument. Where there was an argument to win, he was determined to win it and did whatever groundwork was necessary to ensure victory. We also know that the part of his Hoxton training he valued most highly was the feedback he received on his sermons, which would have required an openness to criticism: *a sharp ordeal, yet it was a salutary one*. In Barnet, he describes his trainees as *critical hearers*, who had some influence on his preaching. It looks as though he continued the practice of learning through feedback and dialogue.

In summary, we cannot pick out any particular warts, but with the nature of the evidence we cannot be sure that there weren't any!

HIS ACHIEVEMENTS

In assessing Stewart's achievements at Barnet, we can draw not only on the evidence supplied by Stewart himself, but also the tribute paid by his ministerial successor and his lengthy obituary that appeared in the Congregational Year Book of 1875. First, Stewart's own assessment:

> *The regular attendance at chapel large – the church members about half of the attendance – a large flourishing Sunday School, where none existed before – a flourishing day school established on liberal principles, a thing entirely unknown in the town before – a flourishing Dorcas Society, whose public sales were the attraction and admiration of the town – a Tract Visiting Society, whose agents were the welcome visitors of every cottage.*

We are left in no doubt of his sense of satisfaction and pride (note he refers to both *my* and *our*) at taking on the rector and the might of the Anglican Church:

> *Dissent respected – our position recognised – our countenance courted – my ministry at Bible meetings, Infant School Meetings, on a par with the clergymen, while my connexion with the young men of the town and the Mechanics' Institute placed me above them in the general estimation of the town.*

His successor confirmed the inroads Stewart had made on the granite rock:

> *He not only effectually served his own Generation, in the work of the Ministry, but he paved the way for those who came after him. The ignorance and self-righteousness of*

former days was in great measure removed by his clear and faithful exhibition of the Doctrines of the Cross.[63]

Finally, his obituary traced his success back to the way he responded to his experiences on the colliers to Plymouth and in the prisons of Napoleon:

It was when inured to the great privations of the early years that he laid broad and deep those habits of industry and self-command which, when in after years sanctified by religion, formed the strength of his character and secured his success.... He was a true man, and men knew they could trust him.[64]

THE STORY OF REVIVAL AND MORAL REVOLUTION

The second story, of revival and moral revolution, is better known but one that, in my view, significantly underplays the role of the Nonconformists. Our image of the Nonconformist minister is still shaped by Victorian fiction: either a pedant of little presence or a self-serving hypocrite. A more charitable interpretation, based on portrait photographs of the senior figures and the minutes of their lengthy meetings, might characterise them as worthy, sober and dull. Alexander Stewart and the young men he helped train for the Congregational ministry tell a very different story: one of dedicated ministers full of energy, intellectual rigour and emotional depth, fired up by a driving sense of moral purpose.

The Nonconformist revival was well under way by the time Stewart took on Barnet in 1823. The Evangelical churches were still on the rise, confident of their mission. What was enabling this to happen were ministers like Stewart, who succeeded in attracting new worshippers and building loyal congregations. His work as a minister throws a spotlight on the dynamism and confidence of Nonconformity, which were crucial to its revival and influence.

FERTILE TIMES

It helped that the ministers and their churches were living in fertile times. George Kitson Clark, in his 1960 Ford lectures, pointed out that:

> *Probably in no other century, except the seventeenth and perhaps the twelfth, did the claims of religion occupy so large a part in the nation's life, or did men speaking in the name of religion contrive to exercise so much power.*[65]

The expanding middle ranks of society were, in particular, seeking a religious framework that would give sense and meaning to their lives. Horace Mann, the young organiser of the 1851 religious census, provided a trenchant class analysis to explain why half the nation was going to church and the other half wasn't. The industrial working class was preoccupied with day-to-day survival:

> *they were not going to waste their energies required for the present by a preparation for remote, and merely possible contingencies.*

The middle class in very different material circumstances had:

> *no doubt of the fact of a future life and spent much of their present life preparing for it.*[66]

A more sophisticated class analysis identifies as lower middle class that category which lies between the working class and middle class: here we may include skilled artisans, tailors, cobblers, sadlers, harness-makers, printers, and clerks, shopkeepers, drapers, teachers and, indeed, Nonconformist ministers. As we can see from the table below, drawn from Robert Allen's analysis, this group was growing rapidly in the first half of the nineteenth century.[67]

Distribution of families or households (%)		
	1798	1846
Landed	1.3	1.3
Bourgeoisie	3.2	8.6
Lower Middle	8.6	15.4
Farmers	10.8	5.7
Workers	61.1	61.4
Cottagers & Paupers	14.9	7.6

The population of England had doubled from 8.3 million in 1801 to 16.92 million in 1851. Broadly, the percentage share of that increase had doubled for the middle class (bourgeoisie and lower middle) whilst remaining similar or declining for the other social categories. Mann was right to say that the middle class in the main accepted the fact of a future life. The bourgeoisie were more likely to prepare for it in an Anglican church; the lower middle class in a Nonconformist chapel where they were made to feel welcome, as if it were their place of worship.

Dissent, as Timothy Larsen has pointed out, *was particularly attractive to the aspiring middle classes who found in it – in addition to meaningful spirituality – community, identity, respectability (in comparison to the non-religious) and habits of living conducive to social mobility.*[68]

Its attractiveness to the burgeoning middle class was both recognised and welcomed at the time by many within the Congregational community, as Larsen illustrates with three examples. First, the Congregationalist historian Robert Vaughan noted in 1838 that:

Congregationalism still finds the body of its adherents among the middle class... that part of the community which all wise men regard as the most sound – as having in it much the larger portion of real social health.[69]

Second, Thomas Binney, Chairman of the Congregational Union, declared in 1848:

Our special mission is neither to the very rich nor to the very poor. We have a work to do upon the thinking, active, influential classes.[70]

His third example is Joshua Wilson, whose address to the Congregational Body in 1862 put the mission clearly in class terms:

Our special vocation is to the middle classes of the people.[71]

We saw from Barnet's example that Stewart indeed did welcome the poor to his chapel, but treated them as a separate category, distinguishable most likely by dress, and he gave them a plain tea.

THE CONGREGATIONAL OFFERING

The godly community that Stewart built in Barnet gives us a rich insight into what Congregationalism was offering to *the middle classes of the people*, or, at least, the lower part of them. The Congregationalists had sensibly moved away from what Stewart called *high Calvanism*, which left no role for human will in salvation: the omnipotent deity had ordained who was to be saved and who was to be damned regardless of how you lived your life. This did not square with the experience of conversion, renouncing sin and turning to Christ as one's saviour. As we saw with Robinson, Stewart was strongly opposed to *high Calvanism* and quick to challenge it amongst his students.

Where, then, was the notion of hell in contemporary Nonconformist Evangelical thought? Michael Watts described the doctrine of hell as:

> *The churches' most effective recruiting sergeant... There can be little doubt that fear of hell was one of the chief factors in the success of the Evangelical revival of the eighteenth and early nineteenth centuries.*[72]

Some preachers, like the Baptist Charles Haddon Spurgeon, continued to dwell on hell well into the second half of the nineteenth century, expounding in graphic detail the precise nature of the torment that awaited both body and soul for those assigned to eternal damnation.

However, this was becoming less and less common. As far as Stewart was concerned, the only mention of hell in his writing is to the *hell on earth* he endured in the prison in Bitche. For him, the Evangelical experience was about the joy of redemption, the urgency of the work to be done and the anticipation of life everlasting. This focus was reflected in the 1833 Congregationalist Declaration of Faith, where there is little reference to the fate of those who did not follow Christ beyond the statement that on the Day of Judgement, Christ:

> *will divide the righteous from the wicked, will receive the righteous into 'life everlasting' but send away the wicked into 'everlasting punishment.'*[73]

27. *Charles Haddon Spurgeon preaching at the Crystal Palace, 1857, in front of 23,000 people. The occasion was the day of national humiliation and prayer called for by Queen Victoria in response to the atrocities of the Indian mutineers and the savage reprisals of the British army.*

Once the issue of the afterlife had been resolved in people's minds, what mattered was how they lived their lives. The answer, as we saw from the examples of the Baptists in Liverpool and the Congregationalists in Barnet, was through study, application and dissemination of the Bible, and through good works in the community.

Society was changing at an unprecedented rate, whether through expansion and the rise of the industrial towns or, more rarely, through decline, as in Barnet, with the coming of the railways at the expense of the coaching trade. Trade fluctuations were common and there was no welfare state: only the workhouse for those who had fallen on hard times. The Nonconformist communities embodied the Protestant work ethic whilst providing a sense of collective purpose and communal fellowship. With the quality of preaching ministers, educated through the dissenting academies and the training schools like Hoxton, it was not surprising that Evangelical Nonconformity appealed so strongly to the lower middle class in particular, as well as to many aspiring members of the working class.

CROSS-CLASS ALIGNMENTS

Puritanism of the sixteenth and seventeenth centuries had appealed to the same social class as their Nonconformist successors: what Christopher Hill called *the industrious sort*, with then more yeomen farmers and fewer clerks.[74] However, access to the power, which Kitson Clark referred to, would only have been possible with the involvement of at least a section of the ruling class. It was the Puritan landowners who made possible the Puritan revolution of the mid-seventeenth century, as England's ruling class was broadly split down the middle. Faced with the threat to social order and hierarchy that followed the Civil War and then the end of monarchy, many Puritan landowners took fright at Cromwell's army rule, supported the return of the monarchy and made their peace with a much narrower, less tolerant Anglican Church. The saints had been routed as the landed classes healed their divisions and reasserted their authority.

Likewise, the moral transformation of the nineteenth century would not have become embedded in the nation's culture without a significant section of the landed class working alongside and in the same direction as the lower middle class Evangelical Nonconformists.

In fact, there were two quite distinct alignments or cooperative ventures involving the Nonconformists and different sections of the landed class. One alignment was between the Nonconformists and the Whigs. The new, serious-minded Whig leadership of 1830 had set in motion the dismantling of the Restoration Settlement of 1662, which had seemed to be cast in stone. This opened the way for the Nonconformists to challenge the Church of England and for the middle classes, with a different moral perspective, to demand and receive at least a share in the government of the nation.

The second movement of congruence was over religion, where the Evangelical drive to spread the word of God brought both upper-class Anglicans and lower-middle-class Nonconformists together. With the aristocratic Whig leadership in the ascendant, this took a particularly dramatic and powerful form in the successful movement to abolish slavery.

Both of these aligned movements pointed in the same direction of moral reform – the holy grail of Nonconformity since the Puritan mission of the late sixteenth century to spread the gospel to the dark corners of the land. The key challenge was to get both individuals and the nation to move from the question that had dominated the long eighteenth century of *how do I* (or we as a nation) *want to behave* to satisfy my needs and advance my interests, to the question of *how ought I* (or we as a nation) *to behave*. Once the changed behaviour had become embedded, the two questions merged into one statement: how I want to behave is how I ought to behave, which is how I do behave.

At the national level, the legislation to abolish slavery was an extraordinary example of the moral argument trumping economic self-interest. On a local level, this question of *how ought I to behave* was being tackled by Evangelicals, whether in the churches of Liverpool, Barnet or Clapham. What was new in the mid-Victorian period was that the question was now being asked (and answered) in the public schools of England.

THE PUBLIC SCHOOL REVOLUTION

In the early nineteenth century, many public schools were, in Simon Heffer's words, *dens of buggery and bullying.*[75] By the mid-nineteenth century, they were striving (and it appears, in considerable measure, succeeding) to be centres of excellence in producing intelligent young men of upright character and moral rectitude who would serve God and their country. Thomas Arnold had initiated the revolution at Rugby School, where he was headmaster from 1828 to 1842. It spread to the established public schools and the cluster of new ones designed for the middle classes, like Lancing College, founded in 1849 by Nathaniel Woodard.

Woodard was a curate in Shoreham, near where Stewart's collier had run aground. Like Stewart, he was appalled by the ignorance of the sea captains. They had, in his own words, *charge of a very considerable property and not a few lives* but *were so ignorant of the art of navigation as to be unable to use the quadrant.*[76] This was one graphic example of a general crisis of ignorance and absence of moral fibre. His solution was to set up Anglican boarding schools for the middle classes, many of whom were having to send their sons to what he called *vulgar, flashy boarding schools* where most of the teachers were *persons who had failed in other pursuits.* In *A Plea for the Middle Classes*, published in 1848, the year of revolutions in Europe, Woodard urgently asked for funding for two types of school: the first for *the higher kind of tradesmen, professional men and gentlemen of limited means*; the second for *quite small tradesmen or even hucksters*, whom he defined as *obtaining their livelihoods by their dealing with the poor.* He wrote:

> *The political and moral well-being of the country depend on the middle classes... the strength of England... and that by neglecting them you can neither have sound*

legislation, peaceable parishes, nor the children of the poor successfully instructed.[77]

He was extraordinarily persistent and persuasive in his fundraising. By the time of his death in 1891, there were eleven Woodard schools, catering mainly for the first group he identified, what he called *the upper portion of the middle class*. The jewel in the crown was Lancing College, whose gothic chapel is the probably the largest school chapel in the world.

28. *Lancing College Chapel. Its foundation stone was laid in 1868 and the main structure finally completed in 2020.*

PARALLELS BETWEEN ARNOLD AND STEWART

What is fascinating, and revealing, for those with an interest in Alexander Stewart, is how similar his views are on education to those of Thomas Arnold. Arnold declaimed:

What we must look for here is first religious and moral principle; 2ndly gentlemanly conduct; 3rdly intellectual ability.[78]

Stewart, as we saw, identified four key priorities:

Early training of mental faculties, moral feelings, social habits and religious sentiments.

Arnold's predominantly classical curriculum was considerably narrower than Stewart's but the emphasis on cultivating intellectual enquiry through dialogue was similar, with student presentations followed by questioning. With both, there was a striving for academic excellence. With both, moral education was at the centre. The question of *how ought I to behave* was at the heart of Arnold's twenty-minute sermons to the whole school on Sunday afternoon; just as it was with Stewart's preaching on Sundays and his assemblies for his scholars. The memory of these intense experiences stayed with their audiences. Years after Stewart left Barnet, one of his original congregation remembered his first sermon: "I am come that you may have life and that more abundantly." In *Tom Brown's School Days*, Thomas Hughes describes the response of the boys to Arnold's sermons:

We listened, as all boys in their better moods will listen... to a man who we felt to be, with all his heart and soul and strength, striving against whatsoever was mean and unmanly and unrighteous in our little world... the warm living voice of one who was fighting for us and by our sides, and calling on us to help him and ourselves and one another.[79]

29. Thomas Arnold. This 1839 portrait by Thomas Phillips was painted eleven years after Arnold became headmaster of Rugby School. He died of a heart attack in 1842, aged forty-six.

MORAL REVOLUTION

Simon Heffer in *High Minds* sees what was happening to the public schools as a key influence in the moral change that:

transformed a wealthy country of widespread inhumanity, primitiveness and barbarism into one containing the germs, and in some measure the evidence, of widespread civilisation and democracy. A sense of earnest disinterested moral purpose distinguished many politicians, intellectuals and citizens in mid nineteenth century Britain, and drove them to seek to improve the condition of the whole society.[80]

We have argued here that this moral revolution was well under way before the mid-nineteenth century. At a national level, the Whigs personified the new approach in 1830 whilst the Nonconformist Evangelicals had been creating for some time a groundswell in their own communities. By the 1850s, we have the upper classes asking the same question through the public school revolution as the lower middle classes in their chapels had been asking: how ought I to behave? It was this alignment across the classes that changed the moral landscape of Victorian Britain.

If we leave it there, we may well go away with a misleading picture of the moral reformers. In his book *Godliness and Good Learning*, David Newsome challenged common misconceptions about the public schools at the time of Arnold:

It was not really until the 1860's and 70's that schoolmasters began to give their official encouragement to organised games and to see in them a great force in 'character-building.'[81]

30. 'Muscular Christianity' a hundred years on?
Lancing College 1st X1 train with Aston Villa in the shadow of the college
chapel, 8th March 1962. The author is the third white shirt from the left.
According to Basil Handford, the headmaster, John Dancey, did not like the
change of kit from the old heavy shorts and shirts instigated by the football
coach, Ken Shearwood.[82]

Instead, Arnold and his peers encouraged the boys to make use of their leisure time with nature walks, observations of historical monuments, and vigorous discussions of seminal books and collections of poetry, especially Wordsworth and the English Romantics. Far from bottling up their emotions, Newsome refers to their:

> *tendency to emotionalism and passionate friendship. The doctrine of the stiff-upper-lip was no part of the public school code of the Arnoldian period. This gradually came in with the manliness cult of the 1870's and 1880's.*[83]

Again, one is drawn to parallels with Stewart and the godly community at Wood Street. With Stewart, we saw the ease with which he spoke about his emotions, how deeply he felt about the loss of his children and his sister, and how he shared that with his family, even his very young children. We saw, too, how twice when responding to Lizzie about the death of Ann, he was so overcome by emotion, he had to change the subject. We also read about the close friendships he had with young men, from his fellow prisoner Frank Finn to some of his ministerial trainees, such as Edward Sherley, whose letters he could not bear to burn with his own hands.

LINKS WITH ROMANTICISM

If this was the age of Evangelicalism, it was also the age of Romanticism. In an essay published in 1955, George Kitson Clark pointed out that both movements were borne out of a shared reaction against the rationalism and materialism of the eighteenth century.[84] Reason had been elevated over emotion and imagination; morality had been sacrificed to utility and profit. More recently, in 2022, Andrea Wulf has traced the origins of the Romantic Movement to a group of intellectuals in Jena in the 1790s. Philosophers and poets, artists and scientists, they called for the liberation of the self to unleash human potential from traditional restraints and material preoccupations. In particular, they called on the post-French Revolution citizenry to imagine and seize the possibilities open to humanity; to experience and appreciate the grandeur and beauty of nature; to explore their own inner world, cultivate their emotions and nurture relationships. With liberation came moral responsibility. As Wulf points out, Johann Gottlieb Fichte, the founding philosopher of Romanticism:

always insisted that our freedom was tightly interwoven
with our moral obligations… freedom always brings along
its twin: moral duty.[85]

There is much here in the Romantic outlook with which Stewart would have been in sympathy. We catch a glimpse of his own predisposition to Romantic sensibility when he describes the valley he entered two days after he had escaped in disguise from Briançon, still a prisoner:

We came to a Valley which had been recently swept by a
dreadful rush of the melting snow from the mountains. I
never witnessed such a sight before, and probably never
shall again. It seemed as if an ocean torrent had ploughed
the valley for years. The bottom was chiefly lined with
large scoured gravel, often in great furrows, with mighty
blocks of granite, in appearance as if just washed by an
inundation of the sea in a storm, dashed against whose
bases lay dead wolves and other animals. The scene was
sublime. As I walked through the mighty valley, and lifted
my eyes occasionally to the Alpine ranges towering into
the skies which enclosed it, I had an indescribable feeling
of my own littleness. Men seemed perfect pigmies.

The Jura Romantics, along with the Lakeland Poets, would not have agreed with the last sentiment, but Stewart's visualisation of the *sublime* Alps, most especially as a prisoner, would surely have resonated with them.

FINAL THOUGHTS

Hermione Lee reminds us that *there is no such thing as a life lived in isolation.* Using Virginia Woolf's metaphor, she points out that the biographer *has a duty to the stream as well as to the fish.*[86] Certainly, we cannot tell the story of Alexander Stewart without opening up the bigger picture of the times he lived through. Nor would we want to. For these times are fascinating, whether we look at what actually happened or, counterfactually, what didn't happen. For example, what might have happened if the Whigs hadn't taken power in 1830, after virtually fifty years of Tory rule, and passed through Parliament the Great Reform Bill, followed by the act abolishing slavery in the British Empire? On a personal, family level, I might ask what would have happened if Stewart had not survived all those seventeen near-death incidents or not had fourteen children?

We can but speculate on the counterfactuals. What we can do with his actual story is to use it to illuminate those times. Stewart lived through Napoleon's bid to control Europe and beyond as a captive of the French. He saw from his prison window Bonaparte's huge army marching confidently towards Russia in 1812; yet two years later, he was walking towards freedom as the allies closed in on the French. In 1819, he witnessed what he described as *the triumphal* return of Henry Hunt to London after the Peterloo Massacre and fourteen years later, in the words of Albert Peel, *rejoiced in the Reform Bill*. He organised anti-slavery petitions, took his elder children to an anti-slavery meeting in London and welcomed William Wilberforce to the Barnet Bible Society.

Stewart was no neutral bystander: as a young man with a political edge who had rediscovered his Protestant faith, he contributed to the cause of reform, which successfully replaced the virtual monopoly of power exercised by the landed class, with their bourgeois allies, and the Church of England. In its place, the Nonconformists and their allies within the old ruling class inaugurated a moral revolution exemplified at a local level by Stewart's treble course in Barnet. Through the life of Alexander Stewart, we can better appreciate the Nonconformist contribution to the bigger story: this was a transformational period in British history, which avoided a political revolution whilst embracing a moral one.

PICTURE
ACKNOWLEDGEMENTS

1, courtesy of Fife Council; 2, 8, 11, 12, 14, 15, 16, 17, 18, 29, courtesy of National Portrait Gallery; 3, 5, 10, courtesy of Alamy; 4, courtesy of Regency Society; 6, 7, 13, courtesy of Bridgeman Images; 9, 27, courtesy of Mary Evans Picture Library; 28, courtesy of Britain Express; 30, courtesy of Mrs Lesley Eastabrook, Lancing College Archives.

ENDNOTES

CHAPTER 1: WALKING AWAY FROM HOME

1   T. Devine, *The Scottish Nation* (Penguin, 2012), 199.
2   Devine, *The Scottish Nation*, 14.
3   L. Colley, *Britons: Forging the Nation* (Pimlico, 2003), 286.
4   A. Herman, *The Scottish Enlightenment* (Fourth Estate, 2003), 15.
5   Herman, *The Scottish Enlightenment*, 360.

CHAPTER 9: TEACHING

6   A. Peel, *The Life of Alexander Stewart* (Allen & Unwin, 1947) 122.
7   J.F.C. Harrison, *Early Victorian England* (Fontana Press, 1988), 135.
8   R. Porter, *English Society in the Eighteenth Century* (Penguin Books, 1990), 167.
9   *Ibid.* 161.
10 Cited in Porter, *English Society in the Eighteenth Century*, 160.
11 *Ibid.* 164.

CHAPTER 10: TRAINING FOR THE MINISTRY

12 Peel, *The Life of Alexander Stewart*, 151.
13 A. Peel, *These Hundred Years* (Independent Press, 1931), 46.

CHAPTER 11: THE NATIONAL CONTEXT

14   D. Cannadine, *Victorious Century* (Allen Lane, 2017), 100-102.

15   J. Morrill, 'Politics in an Age of Revolution', in J. Morrill (ed) *The Oxford Illustrated History of Tudor and Stuart Britain* (Oxford, 1996), 370.

16   S.J. Brown, *Providence and Empire* (Pearson, 2008), 31.

17   J. Coffey and M. Morgan, 'William Wilberforce and English Dissent', *Journal of the United Reformed Church History Society*, Vol 11, No.1 (November 2022), 20.

18   Colley, *Britons: Forging the Nation*, 362.

19   Cannadine, *Victorious Century*, 24.

20   J. Parry, *The Rise and Fall of Liberal Government in Victorian Britain* (Yale, 1993), 96.

21   Brown, *Providence and Empire*, 76.

22   Cited in Brown, *Providence and Empire*, 76.

23   Parry, *The Rise and Fall of Liberal Government in Victorian Britain*, 97.

24   M. Taylor, *The Interest* (Bodley Head, 2020), xvi.

25   Colley, *Britons: Forging the Nation*, 278.

26   Taylor, *The Interest*, 271.

27   Brown, *Providence and Empire*, 79.

28   Peel, *The Life of Alexander Stewart*, 158.

29   Parry, *The Rise and Fall of Liberal Government in Victorian Britain*, 15.

30   J.W. Derry, 'Fox, Charles James', in J.Cannon (ed), *Oxford Companion to British History* (Oxford, 1997) 388.

31   B. Hilton, *A Mad, Bad & Dangerous People?* (Oxford, 2013), 53.

32   R. Brent, *Liberal Anglican Politics* (Clarendon Press, 1987), 16.

CHAPTER 12: THE GRANITE ROCK

33   Cited in T. Perry, *An Independent People* (K. P. & D. Ltd., Metrohouse, 1969), 9.

34   *Ibid.* 8.

35   *Ibid. 10.*

36   Cited in D. Newton, *Sir Halley Stewart* (Allen & Unwin, 1968), 26.

CHAPTER 13: CULTIVATING THE GRANITE ROCK

37   Cited in J. Cox, 'Were Victorian Nonconformists the Worst Imperialists of All?' (*Victorian Studies*, Vol 46, No.2, Winter 2004), 249.
38   Peel, *The Life of Alexander Stewart*, 144.
39   *Ibid.* 147.
40   G.S.R. Kitson Clark, 'The Romantic Element, 1830-50' in J.H.Plumb (ed) *Studies in Social History* (Longmans, 1955), 220.
41   Peel, *The Life of Alexander Stewart*, 134.
42   *Ibid.* 179.
43   E.A. Payne, *The Baptist Union* (The Carey Kingsgate Press, 1958), 78.
44   R. Pearson, *Alexander Stewart's Narrative of his Life* (Unpublished, 2011). For this and further references to Alexander Stewart's family life.
45   Payne, *The Baptist Union*, 76.
46   D.W. Bebbington, *Victorian Nonconformity* (Cascade Books, 2011) 26.

CHAPTER 14: PARENT AND TEACHER

47   Peel, *The Life of Alexander Stewart*, 133-4.
48   Cited in Perry, *An Independent People*, 12.
49   *Ibid.* 13.
50   A. Peel, *Alexander Stewart's Students at Barnet* (Transactions of the Congregational Historical Society 1940-44, Forgotten Books, 2018), 104.
51   *Ibid.* 109.
52   *Ibid.* 110.
53   *Ibid.* 106.

CHAPTER 15: AFTER BARNET

54   Newton, *Sir Halley Stewart*, 30.
55   National Archive, Kew, *Ecclesiastical Census Returns, 1851 Independent Chapel, Wood Street, Chipping Barnet*, Folio 17.
56   Peel, *The Life of Alexander Stewart,* 180.

CHAPTER 16: SURVIVAL, REVIVAL AND MORAL REVOLUTION

57   Cited in Newton, *Sir Halley Stewart*, 25.
58   D.C. McClelland, *Human Motivation* (Cambridge University Press, 1987).
59   S.W. Spreier, M.H. Fontaine, and R.L. Malloy, 'Leadership Run Amok: The Destructive Potential of Overachievers' *(Harvard Business Review*, June 2006), 64.
60   *Ibid.* 74.
61   Peel, *Alexander Stewart's Students at Barnet*, 104.
62   A. Esdaile, *The story of St John the Baptist's Church Chipping Barnet*, 13.
63   Peel, *The Life of Alexander Stewart*, 134.
64   *Ibid.* 179.
65   G.S.R. Kitson Clark, *The Making of Victorian England – Ford Lectures,1960* (University Paperback Methuen, 1973), 20.
66   H. Mann, *Census of Great Britain, 1851: Religious Worship in England and Wales* (Routledge, 1854).
67   R.C. Allen, *The Industrial Revolution* (Oxford, 2017), 62.
68   T. Larsen, 'Friends of Religious Equality: the Politics of the English Nonconformists 1847-67' (*PhD thesis, University of Stirling*, 1997), 18.
69   *Ibid.* 18.
70   *Ibid.* 18.
71   *Ibid.* 18.
72   M. Watts, '"The Hateful Mystery:" Nonconformists and Hell', *(Journal of the United Reformed Church History Society*, Vol 2 No.8 October 1981), 248.
73   Cited in Peel, *These Hundred Years*, 72.
74   C. Hill, *Society and Puritanism in Pre-Revolutionary England* (London, 1964), 134.
75   S. Heffer, *High Minds* (Windmill, 2014), 5.
76   Cited in B.W.T. Handford, *Lancing College* (Phillimore, 1986), 7-8.
77   N. Woodard, *A Plea for the Middle Classes* (Joseph Masters, 1848), available online.
78   Cited in Newsome, *Godliness and Good Learning*, 34.
79   *Ibid.* 29.
80   Heffer, *High Minds*, xiii.
81   Newsome, *Godliness and Good Learning*, 81.
82   Handford, Lancing College, 271.
83   Newsome, *Godliness and Good Learning*, 83.
84   Kitson Clark, *The Romantic Element*, 230-231.
85   Cited in A. Wulf, *Magnificent Rebels* (John Murray, 2022), 350- 351.
86   H. Lee, *Biography: A Very Short Introduction* (Oxford, 2009), 13-14.

INDEX

Carlile, Richard, print of the Peterloo Massacre, *82*

Church of England: Anglican schools, 120; Evangelical wing, 70; and the Great Reform Bill, 76; hostility towards Nonconformists, 97–9; and religious emotion, 69; and the Restoration Settlement, 56; and tithes, 110

Church of Scotland *see* Presbyterian Church

Clapham sect, 70

Clark, George Kitson, 102, 155, 160, 168

Cobbett, William, *Weekly Political Register*, 81

Coffey, John, 72

Colley, Linda, 4, 73, 79

Congregational Year Book (1875), 153–4

Congregationalism: and abolitionism, 78; Albert Peel's history of, 62; appeal to aspiring middle classes, 156–7; autonomy of local churches, 55–6; Declaration of Faith (1833), 158; and Evangelical beliefs, 69; and the London Missionary Society, 70

Dell, Tom, 101, 151

denominational schools, 120–1

Derry, John, 84

Devine, Tom, 3

Dorcas Society, 108, 131, 153

Dundas, Henry *see* Melville, Henry Dundas, 1st Viscount

Dunkirk, 13

education: denominational schools, 120–1; English and Scottish provision for, 49–51; Mechanics Institutes, 107; and Nonconformism, 59; public school revolution, 162–8; Sunday schools, 109

Egham, Surrey, 51–2

English Civil War, 68

Esdaile, Adrian, 152

Evangelical Revival, 7–8, 67–73, 154–61

Fichte, Johann Gottlieb, 168–9

Finn, Frank, 42, 168

Fox, Charles James, 84, *86*

French Enlightenment, 40, 54

French Revolution, 4

Gillray, James, 43, 44

Gravelines, France, 13

Great Reform Bill (1832), 73–7, 79, 81

Grey, Charles, *87*

Haldane, Robert, 7–8
Hall, Robert Jr., 72
Hammersmith, London, 51
Harris, Dr, 60, 61
Harrison, J. F. C., 49–50
Hayter, Sir George, painting of the House of Commons, *83*
Heffer, Simon, 162, 165–6
Herman, Arthur, 7
Hill, Christopher, 160
Hilton, Boyd, 84
Hooper, Mr, 60
House of Commons, painting by Sir George Hayter, *83*
Hoxton Academy, 57–62
Hughes, Thomas, *Tom Brown's School Days*, 164
Hunt, Henry, 81

Industrial Revolution, 69
infant baptism, 109–10

Jay, William, 72

Kenyon, Lord, 50
Kirkcaldy, 2, 6, 48
Knox, John, 7
Krondstadt, Russia, 32–5

Lancing College, 162, *163, 167*
Larsen, Timothy, 156
Lee, Hermione, 169–70
Lemon's School, Islington, 53, 64, 133
London Missionary Society (LMS), 64–5, 70, 132

Mann, Horace, 155, 156
Marryat, Dr Thomas, 88–9
McClelland, David, *Human Motivation*, 148
Melville, Henry Dundas, 1st Viscount, 4–5
Methodists, 69–70, 78
Morgan, Michael, 72
Morison, John, 89, 98
Morrill, John, 68
Mosheim, Johann Lorenz, *Church History*, 55

Napoleonic wars, 4, 19, 22, 26–7, 67
Napoleon, 43–6, *44*
Newsome, David, 166–7